YOU CAN'T TRUST
YOUR OWN MIND

YOU CAN'T TRUST YOUR OWN MIND

BY DR. DAVID J. FRENCH

HUMANICS PUBLISHING GROUP
ATLANTA, LAKE WORTH

Humanics Publishing Group

You Can't Trust Your Own Mind
© 2011 by Dr. David J. French, Ph.D.
Humanics Publising Group Publication
First Edition

Humanics Publising Group is a division of Brumby Holding, LLC. Its trademark, consisting of the word "Humanics" and portrayal of a Pegasus is registered in the U.S. Patent and Trademark Office and in other countries.

Brumby Holding, Inc.
PO Box 1608
Lake Worth, FL 33460
USA

Website: www.humanicspub.com

"Personal Balance" is a registered trademark of Dr. David French

Printed in the United States of American and the United Kingdom

ISBN 89334855-4

DEDICATION

This book is dedicated to my parents, Romulus and Elizabeth French, and my other parents Richard and Patty Howell, also known as "Nana" and "Papa."

I deeply thank my wife, Cindy for the gift of her authentic and her extraordinary ability in being a mother. I thank God for my four miracles: Jen, Ashley, Courtney, and Scott. I have handed off my "baton" to them containing all of my love, truths and wisdom and the map of how to be the best person they can be. Cindy and I remain united as parents and we desired, prayed for, planned and took full responsibility for our children. They came from our combined authentic intentions.

I also thank all of my patients, past and present, for having the courage to share their intimate secrets and pain with me. They have given me insights and the sacred opportunity to authentically share with them. By risking their fears and doubts, and trusting in the power of their authentic, I have witnessed their extraordinary transformation of "reclaiming" themselves.

I am additionally grateful to my professional colleagues and friends for their emotional support, intellectual discussions, and authentic contributions. Their collective feedback, interactions, and moment by moment compassion, helped me formulate the many ideas, theories, and metaphors in this book.

Please allow me to highlight the contributions of the following people:

Dr. Dennis Gowans is a dear friend and colleague of 30 years with whom I share office space. He has given me his extraordinary gift of sound clinical interpretations with very insightful feedback that stimulated me, allowing me to have a more global perspective. He delicately showed me how my passion and excitement would occasionally block my seeing the bigger picture. Dr. D.C. Hadden gives me an ongoing stream of nurturing and soothing support. She is very spiritually tuned in and "understands" the energy that we call "us." She is able to channel it and fuel our personal and professional relationship. Dr. Michael Maguire is my best friend of 30 years and is a gifted physician who believes in treating the whole person. His quiet, steadfast work has attracted hundreds of patients to his practice, making his contribution of what I call "Authentic Medicine." He allows his extraordinary gift of intuition to blend with his superior medical intellect, resulting in a deeper healing of his patients. . . .he actually "listens" to his patients. We have wonderful conversations about God, life, medicine and psychology, and how to authentically contribute to the planet. His two daughters, Megan and Emily, are beautiful, intelligent, spiritually grounded, and accomplished.

Dr. James Pratty is a good friend and colleague who is a Psychiatrist and specialist in addictions. He and I supervise the CareMore Mental Health Clinics. Jim is gifted in his work with addicts and has a superior understanding of psychotropic medications and the rare ability of using just the right type and dosage of medications, achieving optimal success in very disturbed patients. His humor and playfulness give our relationship an added dimension of depth.

Dr. Mark Schnose is one of CareMore's Psychologists and he has given me the combined energy of stimulating professional discussions and heartfelt, God directed spirituality. He combines warmth and kindness with sound clinical judgment to his very successful practice.

Thank you to Jennifer Walters, my Office Manager, for her kindness, loving support, and professionalism for me and all of my patients.

Also thanks to: Joe Weigel, Ed Nino, Jennifer Guerguis, Alma Smith, and Ninoska Ramirez.

Thank you Christine for typing and making the writing of this manuscript fun and efficient.

Thank you Mike and Vickie Roy, and Matt and Bobbie for your careful editing and assisting. Mike, I wrote this in "the groove."

Thank you to the Gyozas: Fosse, Ross, Bax, and Jas for your soft cat motors that provided me with soothing purring and gentle licks during the creation of this manuscript.

Thank you God for my life and the wisdom to get out of my own way long enough to share this burst of creativity to fulfill my authentic intention of awakening those who read this.

THE JOURNEY

I close my eyes to **see** and shut off my mind to **navigate**...

I am on the true path to find what is looking for me...

If I even attend to the slightest distraction, I start to lose my way...

I fall out of faith... My work is to give up this illusion of security and become comfortable with uncertainty. I celebrate my remembering for it is my destiny to share it with all of you.

— David J. French, Ph.D.

March 2010

CHAPTER TITLES

FOREWARD

To know is to predict. To predict is to control.

The machine has materialized. It is an entity that is finally known and whose clandestine and stealth operations have also been discerned. It is not some psycho-cyborg designed to wreak havoc. Consequently, it can no longer control our minds with technologies gone wild. Once it was an insidious darkness and was incomprehensible to the humanity of our species, but now our species has evolved out of a dynamic, organic, light and dark universe that contains this war of mystery, miracle, and mind-expanding consciousness of the human mind.

Metamorphosis is near as our evolved intelligence opens the crack in the cosmic cocoon in which we have been sleeping. As our higher intelligence reaches its critical mass, it will deliver us into the freedom and happiness sought by us through eons of ancient and collective cultures. As their mysterious stories defined them, so do our own contemporary stories, ranging from the hopeful to the apocalyptic, define us.

Science-wielding secular psychotherapist priests came about as a new power to address the human condition of despair, anxiety, anger and confusion. Thus, psychology has emerged as a light that shines in this primordial darkness, a light that has shed understanding on the irrational mind/machine. This new power will facilitate the shift from the unconsciously tormented ego to a new power over this machine. Through the transcendence and illumination of the real Self over this insidious domination of the machine's system , and through consciousness and rational insight into the mystic, mystery and peace given birth by our individual purpose and universal flow, we will prevail.

Dr. French initiates the journey into one's own story so that it may be free to develop and flourish through a new understanding of primitive brain systems transformed into an authentic evolution of our higher brain functioning and into the reality of the clear consciousness and light of the real Self. Simple understanding, education, connection and clean communication permeate Dr. French's perspective and teachings to liberate the Self and put the machine where it belongs: under your control for your highest edification. Hence, your unique contribution to the myriad of individually driven purposes will enable the higher evolution of our species. Our species is on the brink of metamorphosing. Dr. French's Personal Balance Psychotherapy is a therapy that does what is intended, to control the machine that can, indeed, make one's mind feel like it is at war with itself. From this control, the authentic Self can be released to be free at last, and, contrary to Freud's discovery, the ego will no longer be a slave in its own house.

Dennis E. Gowans, Ph.D.

Licensed Clinical Psychologist

ABOUT THE AUTHOR

 Dr. David J. French is a licensed clinical psychologist and licensed marriage, family and child therapist. He is Board Certified in Disability Trauma and Traumatic Stress and is a Diplomat of the American Academy of Experts in Traumatic Stress. He is also a Police Psychologist (Badge 186). In addition, he is certified in Biofeedback. Presently, Dr. French is the Director of Psychological Services for CareMore, a leader in providing comprehensive medical and mental health services to seniors. He incorporates principals of Personal Balance™ in his therapeutic approach, and has a specialized Intensive Program which gives each patient a highly unique intervention in Personal Balance. The intensity of the intervention helps restore the psychic balance, and identifies all the triggers and coping mechanisms that have helped create the person's machine. Dr. French also provides peak performance training to various sales organizations. This particular training allows a salesperson the opportunity to improve their ability to read and assess the more subtle aspects of their client's behavior. Through this training, one learns to effectively "connect" with a perspective client and integrate the art of sharing, rather than selling."

With an emphasis on personal balance™, Dr. French has published professional literature and has conducted hundreds of workshops, seminars, and lectures in the field of stress and trauma occurrences within the police department. Dr. French is the Past President of the Biofeedback Society of California and a member of the Ethics Committee. He was instrumental in establishing biofeedback certification in the state of California and National Feedback Societies.

Dr. French went to Claremont Graduate School where he received his M.A. and PhD. Degrees. In a former position at the San Gabriel Training Center,

Dr. French was Director of Work Adjustment Services where he pioneered the Nation's first computer operator training program for the developmentally disabled. Receiving support from Richard Howell and IBM, this community project continues to place developmentally disabled individuals in responsible positions throughout the industry. Disproving skeptics, Dr. French was the first to successfully use biofeedback techniques with the developmentally disabled as a means of relieving stress. He has appeared on television and radio many times and has been an invited consultant to Channel 7 Eyewitness News in Los Angeles. He has also appeared on the AM Los Angeles Show. Along with his Colleague, Dr. Dennis Gowans, Dr. French has produced and co-hosted the TV Cable Show Stressline.

Dr. French is an avid body builder, who believes in exercise as a primary modality and incorporates both weight training and cardiovascular conditioning in his daily exercise routine. He strongly believes that each one of us is a separate and distinct individual who must take responsibility for his or her emotional and physical well being. He advocates practicing what he preaches and believes that it is important to *live one's philosophy of life* not just talk about it.

Dr. French resides in Whittier with his wife Cindy and their four children: Jen, Ashley, Courtney, and Scott.

PAPA'S ALPHABET TO LIVE BY

By Richard A. Howell

Written for my children, his grandchildren

Always love your family and God's world.

Be kind, loyal and understanding and you will have friends for life.

Courage you'll develop, when things go wrong.

Do your beset everyday and you will grow into all you can be.

Enjoy each moment in some way…even when everything fails.

It helps good times to come back faster.

Find pride and satisfaction in learning how to do your jobs well.

Greet strangers politely with a confident smile and they will usually

Respond in a friendly manner.

Have respect for others if they seem different. That's all right.

You probably seem different to them too.

Inquire of adults the meaning of new words and things. That is the

Only way to grow. Increasing your knowledge everyday.

Jump at any opportunity to go, see and do new things. There are so

Many wonderful places to experience.

Know yourself. What makes you happy, sad, loved, sleepy, angry…

And all of the other feelings that people have.

Then do the things that leave you feeling good.

Learn by understanding what happens to other people when they do

Right and wrong. There is not enough time for you to learn

Everything from your own experience.

Make time available each day to look beyond your responsibilities.

Enjoy the beauty in the people and places around you....

And be glad that you are one of God's special creatures.

Nice boys and girls need to learn how to understand all kinds of

People, so they can tell which ones they trust.

One friend who will be there for you always is worth a thousand others

Who run away when you need help.

Perfection in anything comes from how bad you want it, and how much

Effort you give to get it.

Quiet moments daily keep you balanced in an unbalanced world.

Realize that God gave you a brain as well as a heart. Let them work in

Harmony, open to good things, rejecting of bad and you will

Accomplish most of your dreams.

Senses of sight, tough, smell, taste, hearing, pain, pleasure,

Hunger and satisfaction are the signals to your brain to tell

You what is happening. Keep your body and mind clear of

Excesses of anything, and these senses will bring you through

Life's dangers, unhurt and wiser.

Truth and honesty in the way you see yourself and in your

Relationships with family and friends and most other people,

Will let you enjoy an uncomplicated and basically happy life.

Use all your experiences in the past to help you understand each new

　　　Situation you face. When you are grown up and Mother and Daddy

　　　Aren't there, reach back in your mind, and you will know

　　　What to do.

Victory in life comes to you if you play and work hard. Love those

　　　Who are worthy of your love…honestly and deeply. Believe in and

　　　Fight for those few things in life that are really important, and

　　　Never give up!

Winning is better than losing. Learn from losing, how to win. But,

　　　Don't lose your integrity in the effort to win.

　　　Good guys can win…they just have to be smarter and faster.

Xtra is the word. It means if you give an EXTRA anything

　　　(more than anyone else) you should attain your goals.

　　　Life's rewards go to those who have and give something extra.

You are very special to your family. May you always have something

　　　To do, someone to love and an exciting future.

Zenith is a fancy word for "highpoint." May your life have many

　　　"Zeniths," for there is no end of different fascinating and

　　　Wonderful people, places and experiences that will happen to you

　　　Over the coming years, if you mind your Alphabet A to Z.

FISSURES OF A MIND

Lyrics By James E. Holly

Deep chasms dark shadows the moments of a life

Memories of all the joy all the pain and strife

The mind is a tool to protect from future pain

Sending out a warning when nothing can be gained

The mind remembers all things past sorrows and past pain

All the feelings once felt are never lost in vain

The mind brings back reflections as a way guide

Reflections of feelings once felt now shape a life with pride

The recesses of a mind are held very deep within

Made up of memories including guilt and sin

Dark shadows painful memories from the past

Held within the deep abyss forever they will last

The mind remembers happy times

All things that gave a smile

The laughter shared with good friends

If only for a little while

The mind holds all the triggers all past hurts and pains

Giving fearful thoughts when decisions must be made

The fissures of the mind will sometimes bring on tears

Giving a sense of dread based on all past fears

Deep chasms darks shadows the moments of a life

Memories of all the joy all the pain and strife

The mind is a tool to protect from future pain

Sending out a warning when nothing can be gained

Fissures of the mind a deep abyss of time where memories

Past feeling felt to be recalled anytime

Remember there is a choice to make in all that you may do

The mind is just a tool that may help to get you through

ME

By Peggy Andrus

Revised from Journal of Feelings – September 26, 1990

Who is this person who seems to be me?

As I look in the mirror different strangers I see

When another door of the past is unlocked

A new image of self I do concoct

One still wounded by the dark past

Another who's willing to move into light at last

One kind and loving and willing to give

Another judgmental, fearful, afraid to live

I'm learning not to give into rejection and fear

Nor respond to each innuendo I hear

I'm seeing a new image of self, at last

No longer invisible as I felt in the past

I'm able to feel the joy of living each day

As I move into a more positive way

As I come to know this new person, me

I'm learning to love this new image I see.

"When two people meet each other for the very first time why can't they be real with each other?" This is a question I posed to a large group of ten year olds; a fascinating group of children at Murphy Ranch School in Whittier. I had the opportunity to give a lecture, but rather I chose to have an experience with these young and vibrant minds and eager souls. When I asked that question, the first answer I got was "well when you are real, people think you're weird!" "Yes, that's true," I said, "in some ways that is very true." So I asked them, "How do you protect yourselves?" A little girl in the front row said, "Well, you wear a mask, Dr. French." I said "yes, you do!" I asked them if they all knew that they were wearing masks and I asked for a show of hands. The entire class put their hands up. Then I asked, "Does anyone know the age that you were when you first put your mask on?" There were so many hands up around the room that I had to point to each one of them and ask their age that they remembered this occurring. The average age was about eight years of age. Then I asked them, "What happens if you wear your mask for too long?" That same little girl in the front row put her hand up and said, "That's easy, Dr. French, you become the mask!" Fascinated by this answer, I asked "Does anyone here know the exact moment that you put your mask on?" A few people raised their hands, and I pointed at one young boy, and he said, "Yes, I was at Knotts Berry Farm when I was about nine years old, and I went with my cousin, who was sixteen, and I was really scared to go on the rides but I kept on laughing and my cousin thought that I was having fun." So I asked him, "You didn't want your cousin to know you were scared so you acted like you were brave?" He said, "Yes." What we can see here is a fascinating glimpse into the young mind of a child, and the incredible insights that they all had, especially about the mask and the protection that is needed to get us through our lives.

This book is based upon my thirty years experience as a therapist and it is my simple model of personality that I believe is intriguing and engaging. I will continue to use many metaphors to describe more complicated aspects of the personality of depression, of anxiety, and so forth. My greatest teachers have been the ten year olds. In 1992, I wrote a book entitled "In Search Of the Real Me" (Humanics 1992). In that book, I introduced a basic concept of the two selves. Just like a coin has a head and tail, each person has two facets, two sides. I simply called one the authentic self; and the other the automatic self (the machine). The protective self is the persona, the mask, the facade, the public face, the ego, the shield, the wall, the armor. The Buddhists call it the monkey brain because it is so busy jumping around from future to past skipping over the present in a scrambled attempt to analyze every facet of our existence. This mask, this facade, or as I like to refer it as the machine brain or the machine. This automatic protector, has one important job, and only one; **to protect the authentic part of us.** The mind is like a very complicated and complex computer. Its goal and mission above all else is to keep us safe and protected. In contrast, our "real self" is a more childlike, fragile, and is the vulnerable part of us that continues to be protected because we have the belief (through the mind) that further exposure would result in definite injury, which would be devastating to the self.

What I have found to be absolutely incredible is that many of us believe that we only have one self and if it gets injured and re-injured, it will somehow diminish in its' capacity and size and we will eventually experience some sort of "emotional death." Picture a kleenex that represents the self we are born with. Fragile, soft, vulnerable, and thin skinned. The early experiences of our childhood cause considerable distress, conflict, and pain that gets registered, remembered, and stored by the powerful machine. The mind/machine has a special way of categorizing and storing the information from our early pain and trauma to ensure that this particular event or action will not hurt us again. Each time we have an injury, there is a tear in the kleenex, and continued injury and continued tearing yields something the size of a postage stamp. When this occurs, the machine forms the most protective layer it can. It numbs down all anger and pain. It keeps the self encapsulated in the deepest vault of privacy, so as not to hurt anymore or cause further erosion. Because remember, the death of the self, is the greatest fear of the mind. The loss of self is the loss of identity and the loss of control. The small postage stamp of kleenex remains housed inside for many, many years – a lifetime. There may be fleeting moments where it may pass by the bay window of our home or the screen door of our personality, but never, never, to venture outside for the possibility of interaction; because in interaction there is the potential of harm, pain, and further damage.

The mind cannot risk the loss of self, so it does everything in its power to continue to protect that most precious jewel, our authentic. The protection that is uses is called a coping mechanism, or a defense mechanism. Coping mechanisms are things like drinking, eating, using drugs, working a great deal, using humor to lighten the moment, things like that. The truth is that we have, in fact, an **unlim-ited supply** of our authentic and real self and we can continue to risk, and re-risk and experience emotional pain without really "emotionally dying." What actually happens is that we have a never ending supply of ourselves. For years and lifetimes people live with the strongest conviction that the more they become emotionally damaged, the less there is of them, and that if there is less of them they need more protection in order to ensure that they won't die emotionally, or go crazy, or erode into a pathetic mess of nerves and emotional decay. Many people live with this misconception. The average person believes that who they are is the protection they have become; they believe that they are their machine. This is what I consider the best kept secret of the human psyche.

One of my patients had a very interesting perspective about this. He was a Vietnam veteran who had been in a great deal of combat, and when presented with this particular metaphor he remarked, "Well, Dr. French, you're only dead when you're dead." What he was suggesting is that you really don't ever truly die, until you're dead. Therefore, anything else in life that's emotional, physical, or otherwise; whether as an injury or perception of injury, only results in the temporary experience of pain, but not actual death. Another fascinating discovery along the way has been made in regards to that protective self, or that machine. I particularly like the word machine because it implies the powerful and automatic movement and functioning of this entity, which is totally programmed to do one important thing, one impor-tant mission; **to help us survive**. This machine takes on all different forms and func-tions and during the course of thousands and thousands of hours of psychotherapy and intimate revelations and discussions with thousands of people, I have discovered that this machine exists in all of us. In fact, the majority of people when asked who they truly are actually describe their machine. They believe their machine is them, as I said earlier. So fasten your seatbelt, sit back and relax and allow me to take you into the adventure of the fascinating world of "you" and help you see why you can't trust your own mind.

IN THE BEGINNING

When I was seven years old, I lived in upstate New York in a city called Rochester. My very best friend was Robert Miller. Because there are four seasons, Robert and I would play together in a variety of ways. When it was summer we played a lot of basketball and baseball, in fact, our baseball game was like a never ending game where we didn't keep score but continued to play. There was a large lot down the street and we used to climb fruit trees. Once we were successful at finding a comfortable position within the many limbs, we would pick cherries and spit out the pits. We ate until our bellies were full and we went on many adventures, making our own bows and arrows, digging tunnels, and going on long hikes. In the winter, we would play hockey, build igloos, have snowball fights and cheered when the snow was so high that we couldn't even go to school. One day, I was playing outside of my house and I noticed that Robert was walking down the street with some other boys that I had never seen. It turns out that the boys were his cousins from out of town. As he got nearer, I was anticipating talking to him and I remember how excited I was as he got closer. When he was about six feet away from me I said, "Hi, Robert," and he looked at me, looked away, and kept on walking straight. His ignoring me, or discounting me, was very, very uncomfortable. I immediately felt sick to my stomach and had absolutely no idea why my best friend would even treat me this way. I was only seven years old so I couldn't comprehend what had exactly happened. I am telling you this story because it is an example of how early childhood pain or trauma gets processed by our mind. Remember, the mind's mission is very precise and that is to protect the more vulnerable part of us. In a later chapter, I am going to be discussing many more aspects about the complexities of our mind or as I like to call it "the machine" because it is so automatic. The purpose of this "machine" is to make sure that our vulnerable or authentic self remains intact, because our vulnerability is the most precious jewel that we have in our psyche. It is the "pink skin" of who we truly are. It is the "me" that you are born with, and the essence of our personality and the core of our feelings that are connected to the soul, and connected to God. This authentic part of us is the most precious commodity that we have. Every organism has a defense mechanism. Even the one-celled amoeba, when seen under the microscope will retract, or pull away if touched with a light probe. Whether it be the scent of the skunk, the quills of the porcupine, or the barking dog, each organism must survive within its' own environment. When I went into my house, I remember feeling a sense of emptiness and confusion. What I now know of course to be true, is that Robert wasn't hurting me, rejecting me, ignoring me, or discounting me, he just didn't expect to see me. His mind set and intention was to play with his cousins from out of state. Of course Robert was also seven years old, and he couldn't come up to me and say, "Hey French, listen, these are my cousins from out of town, and I really would like to play with you, but they are only going to be here for a few days, I didn't expect to see you playing outside here, so if it's all right with you, I'm going to continue to play with them and I will see you tomorrow. I love you very much, and I hope you'll understand." Of course, none of this is spoken, and none of this is understood. What happens here is a very interesting phenomena. The pain, or trauma I experienced by feeling discounted , was in a sense biochemically photographed and stored in my brain. The message is sent that I have experienced hurt, and my vulnerability has been impacted because I also felt the physical sense of nausea, emptiness, and hurt. Of course, I didn't understand what had just happened because I was only seven years old, and it just felt like something made me very uncomfortable. There was something very wrong. Now, it's important to note here that this "encoding" by the mind is the beginning of the secret files that it will keep from this point forward as it continues to analyze and interpret all incoming information. If the mind cannot decide between dangerous or not dangerous, it will always pick dangerous. The mind will always take the conservative route when trying to analyze information. Remember its' "mission," above all else, is to ensure the safety of its' most precious jewel, the authentic self. Several years ago, I had the opportunity to meet with my friend Robert as he came out to California on a business trip. He was in Computer Sales and had to come to Los Angeles for a convention. We got together, and after sharing many stories about our wives and children, I asked him if he remembered this incident. When I told the whole story, it was clear that it affected him. With great tenderness in his eyes, and a bit of tearfulness he said, "I have no memory of this, French." The mind will always interpret information and see it as negative, and it will always make it be about us. The reason is that in its' vigilance, it acts like a radar screen trying to collect all forms of information to make an interpretation about what's dangerous or not. In a sense, it's like driving down the street in a car; the mind is at the steering wheel with its' ultimate control and vigilance. The authentic part of us remains in the back seat, very much like a child who is going on a journey with his parent. Now the parent is extremely guarded about taking care of its' child, in fact, the parent has devoted its' whole life to making sure that the child is safe and will remain safe. Remember, what was mentioned earlier, if the mind, the parent, can't decide between dangerous or not, it assumes that it must be dangerous, therefore, the average persons' protection is on a great deal of the time. I would go so far as to say its' on about 95% of the time.

In a later chapter, I will be giving more in depth information about the belief system the mind has and how it continues to build it, support it, and even contribute to helping fulfill the prophecy. For example, any situation that even comes close to looking like a rejection, or being discounted will be interpreted by the mind as rejection. The mind is convinced it is rejection. Every human being has had many types of early childhood pain, disappointment, trauma, or in some cases, severe trauma. In my thirty years as a therapist, I have witnessed and experienced some of the most horrific descriptions of trauma, abuse, physical abuse, sexual abuse, alcoholic parents, parents who were' murdered, children who were murdered, parents who devastated their children, and many other infractions of being humiliated, shamed, teased, discounted, abandoned, and so on. None of us are exempt from childhood pain, because all children experience pain and hurt in one way or another. There are no perfect parents. If an infant is crying for its' mother and the poor mother is in the bathroom vomiting because of a physical illness, and she can't quite get to her baby immediately, that "delay" is stored and encoded in the nervous system by that infant mind as some form of rejection, loss of love, not worthy, etc. Please remember, in the womb, the infant is getting *immediate* nutrition and is in a *perfect* environment. It's connection and dependency on the mother must surely be experienced as "mommy and I are one."

Let's examine, for a moment, another type of injury experienced by the mind, but instead of it being emotional; let's make it physical. If you were nine years old and you fell out of a tree and you shattered your right knee. Of course, you would have crutches, a cast, and go through some type of rehab until you were able to walk independently. Imagine many years later when you are 23, 43, or whatever, and someone bumps into your bad knee. Immediately, the mind knows, that this is old pain that's been reactivated; it's an old physical injury that's been reactivated and is causing us pain in our present day. What is absolutely fascinating is that by contrast when it comes to feeling emotional pain, we are also getting reactivated, yet the mind views it as **brand new pain**. The mind does not experience it as a reactivation of old emotional pain, so the information is encoded and an interpretation is made, in present day. The information is stored, and there's a validation of a belief system based upon the different types of our injuries. Over time, our minds build this belief system based upon countless reactivations of when we are triggered. In a later chapter, I will be discussing the types of triggers that people experience, and the ways that they cover up, or cope, by using defense mechanisms by the mind.

Let me give a simple example, which really will illustrate the very foundation for this book and why you can't trust your own mind. Imagine a work setting where you, Robert, and Linda all work together in close quarters. Let's say it's 11:30 on Monday, and you decide to get something to eat, and you offer to bring lunch back to Robert and Linda. They, of course easily agree, and are pleased with your offer. Two days later, on Wednesday, its 11:45, and you notice Robert and Linda walking right past your desk talking about where they are going to eat. Your mind is now triggered and it's interpreting that Robert and Linda are discounting, eliminating, rejecting, abandoning, or not noticing you. Depending on what your special childhood baggage is, and depending on the severity of that baggage and the number of suitcases you have in your psychic possession, is what will influence the nature of your triggers. For those of you that were abandoned a great deal in your childhood, the trigger will feel like abandonment. For those of you that never felt included, it will feel like you are being discounted, or invisible. I know you get the picture. The interpretation by your mind is the lie. Your mind is lying to you. It's telling you that these people are doing something to you that they're not doing. If you could risk asking them why they didn't ask you to lunch or could you join them, you might hear something like, "No, we're not actually going to lunch right now, we're just going out to the parking lot, Robert has something in his truck he wants to show me," or "We would ask you, but the boss wanted to meet with us and go over something for tomorrows' meeting, that's why we didn't include you." If you would have indeed asked for clarification, you would have felt foolish for having those thoughts and believing your mind because the thoughts are a reactivation of old childhood pain that was felt before you were ten years old. I use the age of ten, because in my many years of practice, and in working with many ten year olds, is the time when most of the early pain or trauma has been stored and a belief system formed – a belief system that is a lie.

Let's look at another simple example. One of my patients was sharing that she was at Starbucks drinking one of those luscious whipped cream drinks. She said a woman walked by and looked at her drink, then looked up at her, looked down at the drink, and again looked up at her, and went into Starbucks. Her mind told her "This woman thinks you're fat, you shouldn't be drinking this." I told her, "isn't it possible that maybe she thought it really looked good and would like to get herself one?" The woman exclaimed, "Why, I never thought of that!" My point, exactly, you never thought of it, but your mind, that automatic protector, that mega machine with its' high vigilance and extraordinary data base interprets it as a negative. Once again, the great lie is being told, and she believed it. I had mentioned working with a lot of ten year olds and how this seemed to be the chronological marker for the ultimate formation of the early core beliefs of the mind. When the mind continues to view everything as dangerous, and when the mind continues to get reactivated, its' interpretations remain negative and fear based. When we continue to stay in an automatic pattern like that, we become more of our mind or our mask. We lose the present moment and we remain shifting from future to past and past to future, in a tireless effort to find some kind of internal security or peace. I will be developing more of these concepts later in this book.

It is my intention to make a contribution to you in terms of authentically awakening you and helping you understand why you can't trust your own mind. Why you have to lie to yourself continuously and why we all believe the lies. In fact, everything the mind tells us that's dangerous with the exception of genuine danger "fire, flood, car accident, physical danger, etc.," *is all a lie.* People are not trying to hurt us, but it *feels* like they are. You might say, suppose someone's in a very angry mood, and they're saying ugly things to us, aren't they trying to hurt us? I would say to you, try to reframe this and look at it as though this person is drowning. They're drowning and they're just trying to stay alive; they're in a really bad place. If you swim over to someone who's drowning and you try to help them, and you get hit in the face, your mind will tell you that you just got hit, that data is correct, but the interpretation your mind gives you is the lie. The person's not trying to hurt you, the person's very damaged themselves, and they're drowning. In their frantic effort to stay alive, they swing out and hit you, you're just in the way of a very damaged person who is in a very tragic place. I will be exploring more of these types of situations, so that I can help enlighten you as to the great lies that all of our minds keep telling us.   Isn't it fascinating how we see peoples' behavior in the midst of a great tragedy. I am reminded of the great tragedies of 911; Columbine; Virginia Tech; the great earthquakes, etc. People are so horrified, and so frightened, and so devastated, that the conventional mind cannot process the horrific nature of what it is witnessing. It cannot do its' conventional job of defending and trying to keep us safe inside. The computer, the great machine is disarmed. The tragedy and all the energy that comes off of the devastation brings us to a place of great vulnerability. Isn't it interesting that in that vulnerability we are unselfish, compassionate, kind, and loving. Isn't it fascinating that we reach out to hug each other, pray, offer great tender comfort, and see no conflict, racism, prejudice, or any other negative interpretations. I don't wish the tragedy on any of us, but I sure do love how we treat each other in the middle of that tragedy. And on a very sad note, once the tragedy has ended, and there's some sense of restoration, little by little people go back to being selfish again; people go back to being defended again; people go back to the conventional protection of the mega machine that continues to lie to them once again.

THE MIND MACHINE:
THE AUTOMATIC PROTECTOR

Several years ago, I authored a book entitled, In Search of the Real Me; Achieving Personal Balance (Humanics, 1992). In this book I introduced a very basic story of The "Two Selves." I described a very simple model that really provides the foundation for this current book. As mentioned in the beginning of this book, all organisms have some sort of defense mechanism. This mega "machine," this automatic protector that we call "our mind," has been called by many other names: the protection, the persona, the mask, the facade, the public face, the ego, the armor, the wall, the shield, the false self, the committee, the noise in my head, the monkey brain. In contrast, the other part of us which is our true or real self is more childlike, fragile, tender, vulnerable, and is kept hidden so as to insure our survival. Of course, when our mind perceives it to be safe we can come out; sometimes for fleeting moments, other times for a bit longer, but most of the time we remain in a defensive posture because the protection is automatic. It's as automatic as a machine would work. It's like an answering machine. When you call someone and they're not there, the machine says I am sorry I am not here right now, but please leave a message and I'll make sure that John gets it. We are hidden from view for the sole purpose of remaining safe. The mind operates with its' sole mission of self protection. It has countless files that have been encoded biochemically, stored with great precision, and are utilized on a daily basis for analysis and comparison.

Let me give you some examples of behavior that clearly demonstrate that your machine is on. Whenever you blame someone else, in any way, that's your machine. When you justify or explain yourself that is also your machine. Many people have difficulty with this description of the mind. Let me give you an another example. If you were thirty minutes late for a meeting, and when you got there, you wanted to explain to the person who was waiting for you why you were late. Let's also state that your entire description of why you were late was the truth. You might say, "There was a big accident on the freeway, and a truck was overturned. Cars were backed up for miles. I tried to call, but I had difficulty with my reception, but I would have let you know I was running late. I did my best to get off the freeway and eventually I was able to take some side streets to get here." Your entire presentation is defensive. People have difficulty with this because they are telling the truth. The issue is not so much in the facts that are true; it's in your delivery and the timing of it. In other words, you are *volunteering* that information to the person who is waiting because you are uncomfortable and feel embarrassed that you held someone up. You might ask, "Well, then what's a more authentic thing to say?" The authentic thing to say would be, "I'm sorry I am late, thanks for waiting." If someone were to ask you why you were late, you could volunteer a piece of information without volunteering the whole defensive explanation. You might say, "There was an accident on the freeway." The mind is continuously defensive because it lives in "fear." Fear and doubt are the jet fuel that keeps the mind firing. Fear and doubt are the main ingredients of what activates the mind because of perceived or anticipated danger. There are two ways we can live. We can live in faith, or we can live in fear. The average person lives in fear, doubt, and uncertainty. Very few have found the way to preserve moments where they can breathe; give pure oxygen to the authentic self and begin to feed themselves spiritually, so that they can really experience the world and the reality for what it truly is, rather than what their mind, or that great machine perceives it to be. The mind always asks this question, "Why?" It always wants to "know," because it's always analyzing and trying to figure out why something is uncomfortable, or why something is not working, or why we're not getting what we need. Remember, that machine has been there since your childhood. It's just like your twin. Just like the coin has two sides, a head and tail, the human psyche has two components; the authentic, and the machine. The mind is drawn to power and control. In its' effort to reduce uncertainty and to deal with doubt and fear, it loves to find ways to control and use its' power to influence. The mind wants to medicate our pain. When the mind is triggered, it immediately covers up the pain so that the outside world cannot know that there was an injury or a vulnerability. Some of the ways that the mind covers up pain is by using humor. A fake or forced laughter, obviously using drugs, or drinking, smoking, eating; especially out of anxiety, or for a need to give yourself internal nurturing, withdrawing – becoming invisible, sleeping, working too many hours to stay distracted so that you don't have to feel any pain, acting out sexually, or being numb, (which is really depression). The mind gets very angry very quickly. It's very reactive. It's constantly defensive, and constantly suspicious. The mind doesn't trust because it always feels betrayed, or expects to be betrayed, or waits for it to be betrayed because its' belief system is it eventually will be betrayed.

Remember, the formation of this mind is based upon all the childhood trauma and baggage that you have accumulated in your life. Many times we find that are common triggers between people; things like being disrespected or lied to, or feeling discounted or ignored. There are triggers that are more specific to people based on that early childhood trauma. All of these things are reviewed in the chapter on triggers. The mind, obviously keeps files on all the people who it believes has hurt it. Remember, there's no brand new pain, but merely a reactivation of old pain, so when there is a reactivation of the old pain and the mind is experiencing it in the present day, it connects the pain of the past to the present day experience and forms an opinion or interpretation that the person, situation, or dynamic in front of them is what's really hurting them, and it assigns it to present day. What is truly happening is there's a reactivation of old pain based on that early biochemical encoding and the mind is merely experiencing the reactivation of it. Because it doesn't know it's a reactivation, its' belief system is that something is happening today, and, of course, all of that is **the** *great lie.* The mind also wants to "get." It is not interested in contribution or giving. It is interested in doing something to "get" something. These are the people who will do things so that they get a thank you. These are the people who will remind you of what they've done so that you can thank them again. These are the people who are looking and waiting to hear some form of affirmation or validation of what they've done for you because they are doing it with a condition or string. They are not doing it freely. They are not giving it freely. They are doing it to get something back. One of the most fascinating paradoxes of the mind is that it is afraid of two things at its' extreme. In order to remain protective, the mind is afraid of everything that comes in on the radar screen that potentially is dangerous or could be dangerous, or seems like it's dangerous, etc., but at its' extreme, the mind is afraid of two things. It *is afraid of getting what it wants* and *not getting what it wants*. What this means is that when you get what you want it feels so wonderful and so good, so perfect, too good to be true, that the mind is suspicious of it. It is also fearful that it will lose it. If you don't get what you want, then you're always longing for it because there's a void or empty space that's trying to get filled. So both extremes are frightening to the mind. The old expression of "waiting for the other shoe to drop" is an expression that comes from people thinking things are too good to be true; that there's going to be an eventual disappointment, and eventual betrayal, an eventual abandonment, etc.

It's interesting to note here that as I talk about the defensiveness of the mind and the percentage of time that it stays on, which, in my opinion is about 95% of the time. What is fascinating is that animals are actually more authentic for longer periods of time, than we are as people. When an animals' defense mechanism comes on, then there is truly perceived danger, or real danger. Most of the time, animals do not remain in that automatic defensive mode like we do. They remain in a very open, vulnerable mode, or an authentic mode, and are occasionally triggered when there is some perception of danger. We, on the other hand, are constantly triggered, very defensive, and mostly living in fear. Our mind goes from looking ahead into the future, skipping across the present, and remembering the past, and in that frantic effort swinging back and forth tells us we are safe. What it is indeed doing is avoiding the present. Isn't it amazing that the mind avoids the present because it sees it as dangerous, and it stays in the past and in the future, where it is actually not *living life*, it is *merely surviving it.*

I am reminded of the young man who died of pancreatic cancer a few years ago. And he was asked that, aside from his wife and children, what was the most important thing to him. He started to answer and the interviewer in their triggered state said "Do you want to travel and go places with your wife and children that you've never gone?" And the young man looked at them with a disturbed expression of disbelief, and said, "No, the most important thing to me right now is to speak from my heart and say what I mean, and if I do something wrong, take responsibility for it and not blame anyone." Isn't he talking about remaining authentic and not allowing that automatic machine to defend himself? Isn't he talking about remaining in the present? Because he is dying, each moment to him is the most precious he has. He had difficulty falling asleep, because he wasn't sure that was going to be the last time he'd close his eyes, or see the walls of his room, or the last time he'd see his children asleep as he gently kissed their foreheads goodnight, was that indeed his last time. In that position, the mind, of course, cannot process the immensity of its' own death simply through this illness. This is uncharted territory for the mind. It does not have a template, or a brochure, or even a map of how to do this. What happens is there is a profound *authentic awakening* because there is now a full surge of energy to remain in the present, to live life to its fullest and to be as open and loving and available as possible with those around us that are the most loved. This man would walk to his mailbox to get his mail and the journey would be each step of feeling the sun on his face, maybe hearing some birds sing, or feeling the gentle breeze across his nose, prior to getting the mail. Getting the mail was the final act. ***It's being there, in the present, it's not about arriving there.*** It is very difficult to live as though you are dying. Intellectually we know that we are all dying, and eventually we all will die. But what we don't do is celebrate the moments and try to strive to clear ourselves to regain control of what's going on ***automatically*** and live more in the present.

There's a metaphor that I like to use to describe how the mind chauffeurs us through life. Imagine the mind is driving a car; our car of life. It's most precious passenger is, the authentic. The windows are tinted and the car is equipped with the highest degree of technology and global satellite positioning available. Our authentic resides in the back seat to remain protected. Our machine is the chauffeur. It's very vigilant and aware of its' position and, of all the possible dangers that exist, might exist, could exist, or do exist. In fact, it drives with binoculars so that it can see way down the road so that it can anticipate potential things that could happen. It's highly sensitive to that possibility of danger, and it's trying to see that danger, even if it hasn't happened yet because the mind knows it could happen, might happen, or it's probably going to happen. It shifts from looking into the binoculars, to looking in the rear view mirror. The rear view mirror represents everything that's happened in our past, all the archives that are there with all the files kept on all those people who have wronged us. All that biochemical encoding that is there to substantiate and feed the machines' very existence. This shifting of future and past continues to fuel the machine and satisfy its' mission to keep us safe and protected. Unfortunately, we rarely experience the present moment. The "present" represents a space in time where we can show up in an open, authentic, and vulnerable state. This state triggers the machine; because the machines memory is that when we were in that state as children and as infants, we were ***extremely vulnerable.*** In that vulnerability, we all experienced some type of early trauma, disappointment, and pain, the very pain that called for the presence of some form of protection by our machine. The ***automatic*** protection of the machine. Remember, it's like touching something hot; you move your finger away in a nano second. You don't touch something hot and think, wait a minute, my finger's hot, I'd better move my hand. In fact, there is no thought at all, is there? It's just moved away automatically. Truthfully, it's easier to stay automatic than it is to be in the present. The mind fears the present, yet the present is where we "live." Fear takes us out of the present so that we end up surviving, not living; yet it takes a dying man to tell us that the present is the most precious place. Why isn't he afraid? Because the horror of his impending and untimely death; the horror of knowing he will not see his children grow, date, or walk down the aisle; the horror of losing his spouse and best friend of many years **overrides** any of the ridiculousness of the machines automatic interpretations. The present is the place of life and it's the place that we return to when there's the absence of the machine. It's the place we started out in; and it's the place that we return to. In the middle of that transition is a lifetime of lying, a lifetime of disbeliefs, and a lifetime of interpretations that have no real evidence; but are merely reactivations of old wounds that once hurt us; old wounds that we never understood have now built up into a reservoir of core pain that provides the foundation necessary to keep us automatic.

In the course of my thirty year career, I've witnessed thousands of different kinds of people with a variety of problems and trauma. During that time I've had the opportunity to help coach and maneuver people into an authentic awakening, enlightenment, and an understanding of how to do the inter-psychic shift of moving the machine over into the passenger position, and the authentic from the back seat to the front to **reclaim oneself**. To drive and hold the wheel again. We can't stop the machine, it's part of us. We can't shut it up. But we can focus on trying to stay as much in the present as possible and learn how to ignore and deal with the constant lies of the machine and misinterpretations about what it sees in reality. There is a resistance of people to attempt to go into the present because each person's machine struggles to remain distracted. There's a fundamental reason for this distraction. As I mentioned earlier, each stage of childhood has a great deal of being present in it. The early injuries that we experienced and the early disappointments, and types of trauma that we felt were all experienced while were in a more vulnerable and present state, therefore, the machine views the present, or holds the present as a very danger-ous place. Because our authentic was injured at that time, we experienced something conflictual and painful while we were in a present mode. The mind encoded it, formed a belief system, as mentioned before, and came up with interpretations that are profound lies. We continue to believe the lies because our belief system has got-ten substantially stronger and more comprehensive; so there is a resistance to return-ing to the very state where we originally got injured, and that is part of the difficulty in helping bring people back into a more present place of existence or at least an opportunity to switch seats from the back seat to the front.

Remember, the average machine is analyzing constantly. By thinking a lot, its' a way of avoiding feelings. A question you can ask yourself is, "If I wasn't thinking right now, what would I be feeling?" or, "If I wasn't eating this food right now because I'm anxious, what would I really be feeling?" "If I wasn't putting this cigarette in my mouth right now and lighting it what would I really be   feeling?" "If I wasn't angry right now, what would I really be feeling?" All these   reactions of the machine are a distraction from the present and an avoidance of the   truth of what we're really feeling. The average person's mind is like a helicopter   hovering over the ground. The distance between the ground and the helicopter is   directly proportional to the amount of pain that one has experienced on the ground as a   child; the greater the pain, the greater the distance in the sky because the helicopter clearing will avoid the very place of original pain; it wants to distance itself as much as it can. Now, landing on the ground is something they continue to avoid because that   would mean they would have to feel and face the pain that is there. The mind is programmed to avoid pain, and seek out pleasure. That is why people self medicate with food or drugs or drinking and so on, in order to numb any sensation of vulnerability.   Our society continues to reinforce this by putting more of an emphasis on the *surface,*   rather than the *substance*. There was unfortunately, a recent news flash about a group   of parents in Orange County who wanted their twelve and thirteen year old children to get breast and nose augmentations. This is a frightening thought, but yet one that is real. Our society considers a successful person as one who is attractive, and making a lot of money. We don't put the emphasis on how successful they are spiritually, how committed they are to their family, and their emotional and physical health.

One evening I was talking with my wife, and my daughter, Courtney, who was eight   years old at the time, was calling me to tuck her in and say good night. She called me several times, and each time I reassured her I'd be there; I started to walk down the   hallway, and my other daughter, Ashley, who was eleven was sitting on the edge of her   bed looking like she was going to get sick. Ashley's room was ahead of Courtney's   room so I walked in to see what else I might be able to do, of course, Courtney was   getting more and more triggered and her little machine was really running saying "Dad, where are you, why aren't you coming in, what are you doing in Ashley's room?," and so on. When I finally went into her room she was massively triggered. She was crying, asking me why I didn't immediately come in; why I had to go to Ashley's room before seeing her, and why I wasn't there when she wanted me to be. I've obviously told all of my children about this authentic and machine relationship and how the machine lies to us all the time. I asked Courtney about her machine being on, and she was very frustrated about me making any reference to that. I wanted to take this opportunity with her as a great learning moment, so I asked her again, if she understood that her machine was really on; and what was the lie that it was telling her about me. She seemed confused and wanted to know what I meant. I let her know that the lie her machine told her was that I went into Ashley's room first, because I must love Ashley more than her. She was amazed and validated that this was indeed what it had told her. I said, "This is a lie and your mind is lying to you about me." She insisted that it felt like it was true. She wanted me to come in when she wanted me to come in and she did not want me to pay attention to her sister first. She felt a sense of entitlement, that she had called me first and she felt that I should have made her be a priority. When I said to her, your mind was telling you that I loved Ashley more. She got very quiet, her eyes teared up and she said, "Yes, it did," and she said "If it's telling me that, Daddy, why can't I hear my own voice?" I thought that was incredibly insightful. I explained to her that the mind was like a policeman. It's always there to protect and defend and keep you safe; but in the process of staying safe, it lies to us about what it sees. I asked her to look at me while she was in this more authentic and tender place, and I asked her, "In your heart, do you believe that I love your sister more?" And she shook her head quietly, no, that she did not believe that at all. This was a great opportunity to show her the contrast between those two entities and a wonderful parenting moment to demonstrate to her the absolute lying of the mind.

There is another story about my children I'd like to share with you . I was sitting on the couch with two of my daughters, Ashley and Jennifer; they were probably thirteen and fifteen years old, respectively, when it came to a commercial, I shut the television off and I was cuddling them both and I said, "If you're ever with a man, or boyfriend, and you *don't feel* what you're feeling with me right now, something's wrong." They both immediately expressed that they understood. At that moment, another parenting moment, I felt very empowered and I really understood why I've seen so many disturbed young girls come in that have had a poor relationship with their father. The father and daughter, and the mother and son relationships are extremely important. The father teaches his daughters about their relationships with men because he's the first man that they interact with. A mother teaches her daughters about femininity, being a woman, being an empowered woman, being a parent, etc. The mother and son relationship are extremely valuable also. It's interesting that the mama's boys; at least labeled by the society, actually make the better husbands, because they have great respect for their mother; they don't see women as objects and as sexual outlets. They view them as sensitive loving, nurturing people that they want to partner with. It's obvious to me when I see a twelve or thirteen year old girl who has been promiscuous or dressing in a provocative way that she's screaming out for attention. It's deeply sad to know that the attention she's needing is genuine love, authentic love and nurturing; but the attention she'll get ends up being sexual, or something in that direction, because boys will easily accommodate that need. It's an illusion, of course, that they're being loved, but it satisfies their need and their thirst, because they are so hungry for the nurturing, validation, and genuine love that they will settle for that cheap approximation and empty affection. In my role as parent, obviously, I've gotten triggered, as my wife has, because it is impossible to be a perfect parent. If we are tired, hungry and impatient and we've tried giving parental direction without any degree of cooperation; the old machine fires up. I've even said jokingly to one of my children, after one of my own episodes of being defensive, "There was a guy in this room a few minutes ago who looked a lot like me and he was not nice to my children. If you guys see him, let me know because I want to have some words with him. I don't like the way he talked to them." They all laugh at that, of course, and it's a very disarming way of saying that's really not me, your dad, that's just a guy that looks like me.

We are all responsible for our machine, and for what it does. Imagine the machine being a big dog we are walking down the street; the authentic part of us is the child holding the big leash of the big dog. Remember, this dog is powerful, smart, analytical, with all the capabilities of all the greatest computers ever built. It is looking for, seeking out, and expecting potential danger. Remember, when it perceives danger, it's just a *reactivation* of the earlier pain, *not* of the present danger that it thinks it's seeing. If that dog starts to jerk forward, we have enough strength to hold it back sometimes, but there are many times we can't hold it back and the dog lunges forward. We stand there helplessly watching as the dog drags the leash down the sidewalk sprinting towards the neighbors' lawn where it is going to dig up the tulips or even bite somebody. Of course, as we finally catch up to it, we apologize for the damaged flowers and for any hurt feelings. We certainly insist it wasn't our Intention; and that we are very sorry for that behavior, but, unfortunately, *we are responsible for it*. It's our dog; it's our responsibility. The machine is fueled by fear and doubt as I mentioned earlier, while the authentic is fed with faith and love. It's the minds' anticipation of pain and hurt that keeps it activated, so that it continues to protect us. It's like the policeman going to sleep with his uniform on, if he wakes up with the uniform, then he's probably apt to protect us better, than if he takes the uniform off momentarily, and wakes up to put it back on. If we keep the armor on long enough, then, of course, we stay protected; so why not sleep in the armor. In fact, why not live in the armor. In fact, why don't we stop living and continue to survive in the armor. Many patients are terrified to face their own fear. They are held hostage by what might be down there or what could be down there. The real challenge and the solution is to *face fear*.

The following is a dramatic example of how someone faced their fear and I would like to share it with you now. This is a story about fear that I think is dramatic, but yet, makes the point about how to deal with fear by facing it. It's the story of a man who had a very bad experience as a child with a mouse. Apparently, he was about six years old laying on the floor when a mouse ran up his pant leg, which of course, terrified him. Once the incident was over, he was highly traumatized by it with many sleepless nights, and the like. As the years went by, his fear of mice remained, Sometimes friends would find out and were very cruel about making jokes about it just to see his machine reaction. One time at a dinner party in his late thirties, someone screamed out, "There's a mouse!" and he automatically jumped up on the coffee table where he was laughed at, humiliated, and shamed. This cruel joke motivated him to go home and in an alcoholic stupor, he set some traps to catch a mouse. He was successful; and what he did next was to face his fear. Remember, I said this was a dramatic example. He cooked the mouse and ate it, and then said out loud, "Who's afraid now?" That ended his fear of mice; it's an example of how facing your fear, can eliminate the hold that it has on you; of course, what are we really doing by facing the fear? We are going through the experience that our mind has held fearful, we are challenging the lie. We are confronting the very experience our mind is telling us is dangerous. We are going back into our bag of garbage, and we are walking through the garbage and coming out the other side. This is everything that our mind tells us not to do; everything our mind dedicates its' automatic existence to preventing us from doing; because the thought of going into that place of pain is everything that the mind is fueled against. It is only when the pain is so horrific, as mentioned earlier, like 911, or Columbine, and the like, that there is an immediate resurgence of our authentic and vulnerable self. The pain is so great that the mind can't possibly defend against it. It is only in that time that our true nature is revealed in its' entirety; granted, it's in pain, but it is really who we are and what we are. Isn't it also fascinating that while we're in that state; we are the most loving, kind, and attentive people to each other. My greatest sadness is that I know what we're capable of, and that we're not able to let it manifest itself. It's indeed very sad, that we can't show that to each other on a more regular basis.

Fear and faith are the most compelling roads to consider; because the road of fear is one we're automatically on, the road of faith is much more difficult. Whatever your beliefs are, if you believe in God, which I do deeply, or you believe in Buddha, or you believe in the great light, the great source, the great intelligence in the sky, or the universe, faith is a more difficult concept to wrap ourselves around because the mind doubts and wants to see proof. The conversation would go something like this; the mind would say, "I don't believe in God." The authentic would say, "But I do." The mind would say, "I don't see God." The authentic would say, "But I feel God's presence." The mind would say, "None of its true, you're being foolish, it's just a story to make people feel comfortable because I have no evidence of it." The authentic says, "It's not a story, I can feel God's presence." You see, they're both in two different states. The feeling state and the thinking state are so close, and so far apart. The two hemispheres of the brain are so close and so far apart; separate by the neuro layer of the corpus callosum, yet the two hemispheres operate so independently. It seems that the machine operates from the left hemisphere and the authentic from the right; yet the authentic is also operated from a very visceral place, a more primitive place of intuition, soulfulness, feelings and sensations. That's why Buddha had a big belly, it wasn't because he was fat, it was because he was enlightened. All the wisdom comes from the viscera, or from the center, from the gut. Remember, when you have a gut feel, you can sense something, the third eye, or you can sense someone looking at you, or you pick up the phone and someone is saying "I was just going to call you." Is it coincidental, or was it something that maybe you manifested? These are interesting questions that we can look at and reflect on later.

I'm going to give you a metaphor that I personally use. Many of these metaphors I've created through the many years of my practice is because I like to keep things simple. In fact, my first book that I wrote, a psychiatrist friend of mine said, "Well, French, you made the human psyche understandable at a twelve year old level." I understand that simplicity is more powerful, so I do believe I operate at a twelve year old level. You can certainly ask my wife, she'll validate that! I'd like to share a metaphor that I personally use when I am triggered and afraid. I'm standing in deep swamp water, which is right up to my nose. I am barely able to breathe, as I look up at the heavens; I am focused on the heavens and in my deep faith in God. I am aware of my blessings, and of the gifts that I have. The gifts that I have are to be shared and brought to contribution. My fear is represented by several crocodiles biting on me. They are not crushing me; they are not chewing me; but they have a hold on me. The largest one has me right by the groin. Remember, I use dramatic metaphors, as this is one that I use for myself. I continue to focus on the heavens and remind myself of God's existence, of my faith, of my sense of ethics and integrity, and of the many blessings that I have. I'm aware of the crocodiles (my fear). I can feel their impact on me. Fear and uncertainty are present, I can't ignore them, but *I don't have to feed them*. The way that you feed your fear is by paying attention to it; by allowing your machine to engage it and fuel your thoughts about it; negative thoughts. Daniel Amen, MD., has an interesting name for these negative thoughts. He calls them "ANTS", which stand for Automatic Negative Thoughts. He's a Child Psychiatrist, and when working with children he uses the image of an anteater that will eat up the negative thoughts and help the child be free from the torment of the negativity. Going back to the metaphor, I am aware of the presence of these powerful fears. I'm aware of the uncertainty and the helplessness that the fear brings; but I don't have to feed it. Being aware, staying focused, staying in faith, staying in contribution, staying in abundance is the way to conquer the fear. Engaging the fear, noticing the fear and then becoming afraid of the fear will feed the fear and then the fueling of that will further engage the mind into unbelievable thoughts of negativity, scarcity, loss, self-destruction, and the like.

I'd like to give you an example of something personal for me where my machine did a big number on me; and of course, the fear got the best of me and for a while

I believed all the lies. I do a lot of body building and I was working out one day. I happened to be doing a triceps exercise when I noticed a lump the size of a small golf ball under my left arm. Of course, I thought I had probably pulled a muscle since I had never seen such a thing. I went to see my best friend Mike Maguire, who is a physician. I asked him what was wrong. He is a very humble and bright man, which is one of the qualities I love about him; and he said, "I really don't know," which really surprised me. The look on his face was that he had not seen this before, which also surprised me and triggered me. This man usually does know. He's extremely intuitive and his gift is being a doctor as my gift is in making a contribution as a psychologist. We are both aware of our callings and we've both been in practice the same amount of time. We absolutely love what we do, and, when he didn't know, it caught me off guard and scared me. I immediately became afraid and the crocodiles bit harder. He said, "We need to have a biopsy taken of it. I'll arrange to have another doctor that I know see you tomorrow." That night I went home in a highly triggered state; my wife, of course, noticed it immediately, even my children sensed it. I said, "I'm just worrying about some things, and I'll be okay." I didn't want to frighten my children and I talked to my wife about it. The trigger became more intense when my machine reminded me that my mother had died at age 46 of cancer. I also remembered that my friend did mention to me that this lump was right on my lymph node. So now, the evidence was there; the fear was rising, the engagement was on, and the negativity and helplessness pursued. That evening, I was getting massively triggered. I was more frightened and more frightened because I was 50 years old at the time. My mother had died at 46; so the machine's evidence was overwhelmingly in favor that this was probably true! My best friend didn't know; he's a great doctor; the lymph node, how my mother died, etc. The next day I went to this new appointment and I walked into the room that was full of people. I signed my name on the register. I did not sign Dr. David French; I only signed David French. The moment I sat down in that busy waiting room, before I could even open the magazine, a nurse opened the door and said, "Dr. French we're ready for you now," which of course, in a nano second, fed my fear. My machine told me how do they know I'm Dr. French, why are they taking me right away? All this, of course is spinning through me with high levels of adrenalin and fearfulness that I've not experienced in a long time. I was actually starting to pan-ic. This is not a state that I am used to being in because I've really struggled to work on exactly what I am telling you about in this book, and trying to live this and be in the best place I can be. This had the best of me. The crocodiles were having their way with me (especially the biggest one!). The machine was dragging me down the street, as I was holding on to the leash. We walked by all of the examination rooms and I was even more curious as to why they were not putting me in one. They finally asked me sit down in a very small office and the nurse said, "The doctor will be right with you." When she shut the door, I felt the crocodiles pull me under, as my machine thought why am I in this office and why am I not in an examination room, and so on. The moment I was starting to feel even more anxiety, the door opened, and it was the doctor. His gentle eyes and demeanor showed me that he had sensitivity and warmth, so I immediately stood up and said, "I apologize, I'm a little nervous right now, but if there's something you want to tell me, I prefer you just tell me straight out." The moment I said that, I could see in his eyes that he had no intention of telling me anything like that, which of course, made me feel self conscious and foolish. I apologized and said, "I m sorry for saying it like that, I'm just very nervous." He understood. I asked him why I was in that room and why they took me so quickly. He told me that my friend had called him and they wanted to give me a professional courtesy! They knew I had my own patients waiting, so they were willing to see me in a very swift manner. We went to an examination room and the first thing he said when he looked at it was, "Wow, that really is big!" which, of course, triggered me again. In my attempt to cover up my fear, I said with humor, "No, you're supposed to tell me you could take it out with a pocket knife right now, and we would be done with it." He laughed a little bit and he said that we would need to biopsy it, and so on. The next day, I had surgery. It was removed from my arm. It turned out to be a lipoma, a fatty growth that ended up being the size of a baked potato! I teased my wife about it and said that we should send out birth announcements and say I gave birth to a baby lipoma. All that was missing was teeth and hair! This is another example of how that machine can take us on a ride where we are being dragged down the street by the very power of its' negativity. Allow me to exaggerate to make the point. I spent 400,000 hours worrying about having cancer, and I spent three seconds thinking it was okay. What I learned from this experience was the power of that machine and how it could have its' way with me especially when I came to a place of panic, helplessness, feeling like I was seven years old, and the earthquake was crumbling in on me. What I also learned is that from this point forward, whenever I was massively triggered and frightened; whatever window of time I spent being like that and whatever images I had, I was going to do my best to counterbalance those images with an equal amount of time saying everything was going to be fine. That's not something we do. We are terrified.

We stay engaged and we listen to the negativity; but if we really try to counterbalance it with positive affirming thoughts where the ending is going to be acceptable, okay and safe, then we overcome the lie and remain in faith.

Remember the ten year olds, they know and they understand because they are young enough to have just begun to understand the mask. They are old enough to where they've been injured and disappointed and hurt, to even have the mask manifest itself. I had a brief discussion with a ten year old once in my office, I was telling him about the two selves and about his machine and his authentic self. He was a very intelligent young boy with a great ability to have insight, so he could quickly grasp the subtleties of what I was saying; so he looked at me and said, "If the machine doesn't protect me, what would protect me?" And I said, "God." And he said with his remarkable insight, "So God is like our natural machine," which I found quite amazing. If we stay in faith, and we're in the moment, we are entitled to the natural protection of God who created us. By living in fear and doubt, we engage the minds' interpretation of what is safe and the mind's interpretation of what is dangerous and we live with the great set of lies that become the map of our existence and belief system. We literally spend the rest of our lives living a program that's based on lies generated from the early baggage of our childhood because of the continuous reactivation of old pain and the interpretation that the old pain is, indeed present pain so that the activation of the machine has to remain. When the mind shows us there is continuous pain, and an affirmation of what it says will happen, then it continues to justify its' own existence by feeding itself with its' own lie. Remember, like a very damaged parent, it believes in protecting its child; it's just not well informed. It's not the brightest parent. The information it is getting is not true. The authentic, on the other hand, already knows the truth. The authentic is naturally protected. We rarely allow ourselves the opportunity to be in the present long enough to return to that state of vulnerability. It is the state of vulnerability that we avoid, as I mentioned earlier, because the state of vulnerability is where we got **originally hurt.** The mind will dig its' heels in and resist any attempt to return to that original place of pain. It does not want to go back there; it does not want to remember there. Consequently, as I also mentioned before, it uses the binoculars to look forward. It's constantly looking forward and its' looking in the rear view mirror. It looks at what might happen and remembers what did happen, and it does not allow us to see what's **happening.** So, in a sense, the present is what the machine avoids and by avoiding it, we are **surviving** life, not **living** life. Because we are mistrustful, we listen to the many lies of our mind and we always believe it's' interpretation. You cannot trust you own mind. It will lie to you in an attempt to protect you and by believing it; you are rejecting the very source of what created you because you are not allowing that natural protection to be there. The point is, the machine looks strong; but it is actually very weak. The authentic looks weak; but its' incredibly strong. Vulnerability is strength, vulnerability is courage. The bigger the armor, the greater the machine, the greater the lies. The machine is like a movie set, you drive by it looks like a brick building, but when you go up to closely examine it, you realize it's held up by two by fours. It's all frontage. It is not genuine brick. It gives the illusion of brick and it gives the illusion of strength; yet the true strength is in our vulnerability. When a child speaks, or one speaks from one's heart, that is our vulnerability because vulnerability is clean, pure, and honest. Vulnerability is what we are when the machine is momentarily not engaged in the future or past – when we choose to stay in faith and belief.

When the trauma is great, when the trauma is severe as in the case of molestation, witnessing a murder, and other horrific acts, especially in childhood, the mind breaks into pieces. It fragments in order to survive the severity of such trauma. Years ago, this was called Multiple Personality Disorder, today in psychiatry we refer to it as Dissociative Identity Disorder. In Dissociative Identity Disorder, the conventional mind that was commissioned to us at birth, breaks into smaller pieces of machine in order to handle and survive the trauma. Each piece or personality has a separate and distinct memory of different aspects of the trauma. The therapeutic process is a very, very long one which can result in many years of treatment at several times a week. The therapist must form a separate and distinct relationship with each part of the personality and then somehow find a part of the authentic that can act as a grounding force or neutralizer to weave and integrate the entire broken bottle back together. Of course, once glued, it will never function the same. It may not hold water or liquid; but indeed, it is a bottle nonetheless. Patients can survive and continue on with their lives although many aspects of their lives are greatly impaired such as sexual and intimate relationships, and so on.

The delusion is another form of masking and survival. When the trauma is so severe, the mind, in an attempt to deal with the severity of such trauma, creates and invents "a new reality" so that it can regain some sense of itself and its' stability. The "delusion," of course, is completely created and done with smoke and mirrors to create an alternative reality. It's the mind's way of fooling itself, once again, another component of that fascinating structure, the mind. It actually lies to itself, once again, in its' delusional state; but it forgets that it lies to itself so that it can survive. The trauma occurs and the trauma is severe, but the organism survives. The price for survival is it formulates a collateral reality so that it can go forward. Remember, the quality of life is compromised because one is not living authentically in any form of the present and one is not living in any kind of grounded or intimate way; yet one is surviving. The bottle is flawed through its' re-gluing and many small splinters are missing, but the person goes forward. The bottle marches forward. The mind forgets that it lies to itself because it has encapsulated the very trauma that has allowed for the formation of its' new reality. The encapsulated trauma gets buried deep within the psyche, deep within the privacy vault of the human condition. The fleeting memories slowly die down into a wisp of smoke; the mind houses new thoughts based on its' new delusion and its' new survival mechanism and it begins to find more evidence that suits its' new newly formed reality. Isn't this a splendor to behold in its' own elegant way, the human mind is the master of deception, and yet the master of creation. In its' own elegant way the human mind is a fortress of security, and, can be, a tormented prison of hell – it is our gift and our curse!

In the chapter on depression, I use the metaphor of a closet. The closet is the place inside where the mind stores all the pain and anger. We are only given so much room in the beginning through our own creation; the conventional closet that God gives us has a certain amount of psychic space for storage. The closet gets filled very quickly, and as we continue to go through our life, the memories of the trauma and the mind's continued interpretation of current trauma and pain, keeps the closet filled. If we run out of room in our conventional storage area, the mind, as mentioned earlier in this chapter, will fragment, as in the case of severe trauma and Dissociative Identity Disorder. In its' fragmentation, the mind shifts its' psychic position for storage and begins to store things in a hallway in front of the closet. We now shut the hallway door, once that's filled, by holding in pain and we begin to use the living room as our closet. When we run out of living room space, we must go outside, shutting the front door behind us, yet acting as another compartment for storage. Now our whole house is used for storage. The mind must take refuge outside. We are standing outside on the welcome mat in front of our house with years of storage behind us as we begin to make our way down the driveway, continuing to throw feelings behind us, not wanting to feel or express them. At some point, we hit the sidewalk in front of the house; and that's where the break occurs, and we lose the connection to ourselves. This is my version of what insanity is. Insanity is the loss of self. Insanity never happens by releasing feelings, it only happens by an extraordinary suppression of feelings encapsulating severe trauma into the inner recesses of the psyche hidden from view; only to give the illusion that there is a self residing there. There is no more storage space, so he mind breaks off in search of more safety leaving the grounding of our home – the balloon flies off in the wind without an authentic holding on to the string.

As I've indicated, the average person's machine, or mind, is defending about 95% of the time. Let me illustrate another facet of this of this fascinating entity by using the metaphor of what I call "the car." I've mentioned that the average person is surviving life rather than living life. Picture the mind behind the wheel of the car; grabbing the wheel and exerting its' control over driving it through life; of course, its' mission is to protect the precious cargo of the authentic self. Most of us are in the back seat, patiently waiting for it to be "safe." Unfortunately, it never seems to be safe enough to come out all the way and the windows are tinted in the back seat so not everyone can always see us; but we can of course, look out, because the mind remains triggered, coping, and surviving. As I indicated earlier in this chapter, the mind is using binoculars to see way down the street because its' anticipating what might happen, what will happen, what could happen, and so on and after its' glancing through the binoculars, it glances through the rear view mirror to remember what has happened, what did happen, who hurt it, why it got hurt, and so on. It rarely remains in the present; where the moment of life unfolds and being alive takes place. This is what we call the "now." This is what is achieved through meditation and attempted through Yoga and other forms of centering and grounding. This is what Zen Masters do to instruct their students to use disciplinary procedures and different exercises. This is where the dying person lives. Now, there are some people who are so damaged, that they have found refuge in the trunk. Their trauma and their history is so severe and so devastating that sitting in the back seat is not safe enough. Of course, there are a few people whose trauma transcends the trunk; the trunk of safety, and they are in a U-Haul behind the car. They are detached from the "now" frozen into dissociative, fragmented pieces. And lastly, there are those who even have been thrown out of the U- Haul before age ten and have the label of Sociopath. The Sociopath has no authentic. They have no soul and no connection to God. They have a lifeless stare where 100% machine inhabits their psyche; there's no remorse or conscience, just a vacant shell of a person – a creature like existence.

In describing the power of the mind and giving metaphors that illustrate its' uncanny proficiency, there is a subtleness of this machine. Please let me give an example of how I, myself learned of how subtle it was in an experience I had. A while back, I was in a mall and I walked by a Godiva Chocolate Shop. I immediately went in and I looked around and ended up purchasing several wonderfully decorated gold boxes of chocolates for several of my employees. When I brought them back into the office, they were indeed delighted and surprised and all of them in their own way, wrote a personal note, or gave a hug while telling me "Thank you." I went in my office with one of them to have a brief meeting, and as she was beginning to get her things together I remarked to her "You really did like the chocolates, didn't you?" She said, "Oh yes, Dr. French, I really did. Thank you again." I felt some discomfort hearing myself ask again, inviting the reassurance of her gratefulness; I realized that I was triggered. She looked at me and I had the sensation that she was aware of my discomfort. I realized I felt a bit uncomfortable and disappointed because I had expected a different response rather than just thank you. The truth is, I wanted them to see that I was being special and say that I was the best boss that they'd had, and so on. However, at the time I purchased the chocolates, that was certainly not my intention nor was it part of my conscious thought. I really believed, at that moment I was just being a nice guy and I was doing something nice for the people that I appreciated and valued in my office. Well, that got my attention, and I immediately had an insight about how subtle and powerful this machine really is. What I am saying here is that the machine had operated on this very delicate level it had done something through its' coping and subtlety to *appear* to be authentic, when in fact, there was a condition, a string, or something attached to the act of giving.

A patient of mine, years ago was remarking about how he enjoyed opening doors for many women. He said one time that several of them weren't grateful, and they didn't even say thank you. I suggested to him that if he truly needed them to say thank you that he really wasn't giving a gift at all. There was a condition; there was a string. Just like the case with my chocolate there was a string, and there was a condition. I needed reaffirmation of my specialness, and I was afraid or certainly perceived it to be unsafe to actually ask directly for what I needed. What I really find remarkable about this story that I've told you, is that we can fool ourselves into believing that we're being genuine, when we are really not. You might wonder how you can truly know. Certainly this is a difficult dilemma. I am clearly aware that I'm triggered when I am acting in ways that are obviously defensive. If I'm angry, confrontational, argumentative, agitated, and so on. It's clear that I am in trouble. And I am certainly aware of the times when I'm exaggerating something or distorting something, even though I may not admit it to all of you; inside I know the truth. My way of saying it is, at four o'clock in the morning we get up to go to the bathroom, we know who we are; we are inside of our own skin. We may not admit the truth to the general public or even to a few friends, but you know who you are.

How do you really know when you are being authentic? The machine can be very subtle and can appear and sound authentic, it can charm and be charismatic, it can speak softly, it can sell, it can maneuver and manipulate. How does one truly know? The only absolute way of knowing about being authentic is if you're feeling pain. Of course, people cry many times when they are angry or frustrated. People cry sometimes when they are whining, feeling sorry for themselves or being pitiful. This is emotion; but it's not authentic emotion. So, when I say that you can absolutely know you're being authentic is when you're feeling emotional pain, I am referring to the true release of emotion that comes from a much deeper place, it's a place of release. Interestingly, if you took two people and put them in two separate rooms and you told one person to laugh as hard as they could for an hour; and the other person to cry as hard as they could for an hour, at the end of that time, both people would appear very similar and even feel the same. They would both look spent. Their eyes would be red, maybe puffy. They both would have cried to some degree through laughter and through the release of pain. They both would have felt a tremendous sense of relief. What's fascinating here is that the road they end up on is the same.

Emotions are made to be felt, they are made to be released; not stored, not encapsulated, not buried in the trunk, not dragged by the U-Haul; but to be released and expressed through and out into the air. When I am in an authentic, loving place, being my real self, I'm far more patient with people and I certainly don't focus on criticizing them or blaming them. I'm far more drawn to the authentic part of them that's usually hidden from view. One thing is true, if you're being the machine with someone it **calls** to their machine. If you're being authentic with someone it **calls** to their authentic. I invite you to start a conversation with a total stranger, and pretend that this is one of your friends, and that you can feel safe enough to take a risk about something personal and you feel brave enough to even share tender, more vulnerable emotion. You will get reception, you will get authentic, and you will get another person joining you. In a way, ***everyone's waiting for everyone else to go first***. You see, we're all afraid of going first. Because if I go first and you don't, then I'm vulnerable and you're not. If I go first and you don't, you get to see me vulnerable and I don't see you, I just see an eye looking through the knothole in the fence. You are still hidden from view; I'm not. You get to see my pink skin, you see me without the armor. You'll know my vulnerability; you'll know my Achilles heel; you're going to judge me, you're going to criticize me, you're going to make fun of me, you're going to hurt me, you're going to abandon me, you're going to discount me, you're going to blame me, etc. I've come up with a very significant and important insight and I will say it to you this way. If you and I are talking and we're sharing for an extended period of time and your machine is on, if you are triggered while you're with me, I am ***clearly*** doing something that's contributing to that trigger. Conversely, if we're together, and we're being authentic, it's because we are both remaining authentic and we're sharing from a very safe and tender place. There is initial respect for that type of sharing. When people share authentic to authentic, there is a synergy, energy, and a flow. It's like bringing two candles together. Person A, Person B and then there's the entity A-B. The touching of the candles makes for more light. But a healthy relationship is not wrapping the candles around each other, its standing as close as can be, staying independent, yet sharing the light. Most of the love songs that are written are not very healthy, "You Complete Me", "I Can't Live Without You", these seemingly adoring phrases that charm many people are not very healthy psychologically. You don't need someone to complete you; it's your responsibility to complete yourself. Each one of us has to "make the cake" inside of us. The cake represents the substance that we are. Each one of us makes the cake, by watering and feeding the authentic part of us. We can receive frosting from many people that love us, but it's ***our*** responsibility to make the cake first. You can't get your cake from someone else. Many little girls thought that the prince was going to come by in what we refer to as the "Cinderella Complex" where the prince would show up and save them. It's your responsibility to save yourself, it's my responsibility to save me, we can share frosting, but we can't make the cake for each other. Too much frosting without a cake underneath is not healthy and you will get an upset stomach

TRIGGERS AND COPING

We don't see things as they truly are. We see things through our mind's interpretation. The" true reality" is not based upon our machine's interpretation, but rather what is existing in the present moment without any imposition of any type of interpretation or analysis. This is what a trigger is all about. A trigger is some kind of action, or circumstance or event that reactivates our earlier pain and is continuously interpreted by our machine as dangerous. An immediate protection is formed based upon that interpretation. It's a stimulus that sets off an immediate and oftentimes unconscious reaction. We all get triggered hundreds of times each week. We experience something as real, or imagined, or an anticipated loss, where we don't feel safe, loved, and our well being is put in jeopardy. Over the years, I have recorded hundreds of different triggers that patients have identified in the course of their therapy. Many of us have the same triggers, because we have common childhood pain and trauma. A list of these triggers is forthcoming in this chapter.

The brain and spinal cord make up the major part of what we call the Central Nervous System, "CNS." Since the beginning of time, the human species has depended upon the CNS to assist in its' protection, defense, and ultimate survival. Hundreds of studies have indicated and shown that the nervous system is composed of an extraordinary network of neurons. The brain interprets information based upon its' previous associations and relationships. When the brain perceives danger, for example, information is sent by the way of the spinal cord to various target areas in the body. The information is sent biochemically and various electromagnetic changes occur on a cellular level to activate specialized nerve cells for preparation of what the brain has perceived to be "dangerous." For example, imagine you are walking down the street on a warm and sunny day, (and you are being telemetrically monitored where your physiology is being recorded at a remote location by way of computer). A baseline would be taken of your resting heart rate, muscle tension, sweat gland activity, brain wave activity, etc... You reach a particular corner, and as you begin to step off the curb, a large diesel truck screeches on its' brakes and honks its' horn. What is happening precisely at this moment is relatively basic:

1) Your pupils dilate

2) Your heart rate increases substantially pumping blood to the larger muscles and to your brain

3) Dryness occurs in your mouth

4) Blood leaves your periphery (hands and feet) so that your extremities are cool

5) Your brain wave activity shifts into a much faster state

6) Your respiration rate increases substantially while small hairs on the back of your neck stand erect

7) Your overall muscle tension increases in your forearms, forehead, trapezoids' and abdominal area

8) Your blood pressure rises considerably

9) The sympathetic response of your CNS is fully activated

These are the primary reactions to the perceived danger that are wired automatically. There are more intrinsic reactions to the perceived danger. There are more reactions of a biochemical nature that are not relevant to this discussion. Traditionally this is known as the "fight," "flight," or "freeze" reaction. The body must flee, fight, or be paralyzed by the perceived danger. This response is genetically wired into us prior to birth. It has been wired into the human organism since the beginning of our existence on this planet. Many other responses are wired into the organism. For example, a puff of air into the eye will cause an immediate eye blink; throwing a projectile at someone will illicit an immediate arm and elbow up defensive reaction; touching someone from behind may cause a tactile or defensive response. Basically, the body is protecting itself against danger. This is the basic, primitive machine at work. We also know this happens on a cellular level when there's an injury. If you cut your knee, for example, it will begin the process of healing through the body's normal defense reaction. Later the scar will form, revealing proof through the tissue that a defense has occurred. This is basically a physiological manifestation of the minds' activity. It' is a physiological state of being "triggered." The mind is constantly interpreting incoming information to decide whether or not there are threats. If the mind cannot decide between dangerous or not; it will always pick dangerous. It will always take the conservative route. It will never put us at risk. The mind does this automatically and the interpretation or the reaction that it has is what we refer to as being triggered. The triggered response always results in the form of behavior that allows us to cover up or cope, and survive the pain. There are many different behaviors that we use to cover up pain. Once we're triggered, some of us become quiet, confrontational, defensive, and argumentative, others of us will eat food out of anxiety, or have a drink, or smoke a joint, want to isolate socially, or be distracted by working a lot of hours, etc. Sometimes we use humor to bring levity into a more serious situation. Others of us smile with the automatic "airline stewardess" smile that may bring a sense of calm into what has previously been an uncomfortable situation. Our mind/machine continues to decide what's dangerous and each decision it makes is what we refer to as a trigger, followed by a coping or surviving behavior. The following list is an accumulation of actual triggers that people have described over the thirty years of my clinical practice – see what ones fit you:

- people leaving or any kind of separation

- when people question my feelings

- when people make me wrong or blame me for something

- insensitive people or rude people

- any type of injustice or unfairness

- feeling disrespected or not feeling valued or honored

- not being taken seriously

- people not trusting me or believing me

- people lying to me

- people taking me for granted

- when people treat me out of convenience rather than being genuine with me

- wanting my space to be honored

- any form of prejudice or racism

- any type of disrespect or abuse to the elderly or the disadvantaged

- any surprises

- feeling blamed

- anything racial

- whenever I see anger or rage

- success or feeling successful

- not being given credit

- any type of disagreement or confrontation

- anytime somebody is in opposition with me

- feeling frustrated

- being interrupted

- not understanding

- closeness

- perceiving success or failure

- anything sexual

- deadlines

- having more to do than I can deliver

- feeling like I'm not enough

- any type of isolation or loneliness

- someone making a joke or having a crowd laugh at me

- feeling inferior or discounted

- any loud noise or raised voice

- being told what to do

- feeling challenged

- feeling I have to say something

- constantly being compared to other people or siblings

- feeling sad

- being faced with a decision

- feeling rejected

- feeling misunderstood

- things not being clear

- any form of disrespect

- someone not following the rules

- being ignored

- being challenged

- when things move too slowly

- when things don't happen according to plan; especially my plan

- feeling like I don't belong

- being controlled

- feeling alone

- feeling manipulated

- not feeling safe

- being told I'm stupid

- lying

- someone overseeing my work or second guessing me

- anyone pretending

- a lack of control

- being vulnerable

- money

- over care taking

- looking wrong

- curiosity

- people not taking my feelings into consideration

- not being heard

- people being guarded

- being patronized

- anyone critical or direct

- arrogance

- rudeness

- being boxed in

- people not being straight with me

- when it seems I don't matter

- any form of public acknowledgement

- when someone denies or postpones making love with no apparent reason

- when someone acts like they don't know what I'm talking about even after I explain myself several times

- when people take sides, especially against me

- any type of laziness

- when someone implies that my sex drive is abnormal

- when I get interrupted at work because of someone needing something from me

- when someone exaggerates a situation or a story they're telling

- when I see my wife being overly friendly with other people or other men

- when people put me on the spot, especially in front of other people

- someone walking out during an argument

- when someone looks at me like they hate me or is disgusted with me

- when someone tries to act tough in front of me but treats me differently when I'm alone with them

- when someone won't forgive me

- when people don't follow instructions

- when someone makes mistakes due to a lack of effort

- when I have to do other peoples' jobs

- when someone thinks that I owe them something

- people who continue to make excuses for their mistakes instead of taking responsibility

- when people pick on people who are less fortunate than they are

- arrogant people

- people who talk down to me

- people who betray my trust

- sloppy paperwork and disorganization

- people who think that I haven't worked for what I have obtained

- anyone who procrastinates

- when people break promises

- people who will not make a decision

- when my children tell my wife and I to stop arguing

- when I ignore my children's questions because of my own selfishness at that moment

- when people are late and won't apologize or take responsibility for being late

- having my integrity or honesty questioned

- when my authority is challenged or disregarded

- when major decisions are made without my consent or knowledge

- when I am excluded from secrets

- when I set a situation up in my mind and then it doesn't occur in real life

- when my spouse doesn't back me up in front of my children

- when people keep asking how I am

- people laughing; picking on me

- constant teasing

- rude, snobby people

- when my children talk down to me

- people who really don't listen

- people who are elitist

- slow drivers

- When people do dumb things (for example forgetting car keys, etc.)

- losing

- bullies

- when people see me as incompetent

- when I think people are thinking something about me negatively

- pretentious people

- sarcastic people

- materialistic people

- racists

- people who lack empathy

- people who don't say thank you

- people who watch too much TV

- going into a beauty shop if I don't look good

- bags under my eyes

- fat on my stomach

- being falsely accused

- when people compliment me

- anything superficial

- being yelled at

- accused of things I didn't do

- people with no sense of urgency when warranted

- lazy people

- not getting my own way

- stupidity

- passivity

- unforgiving people

- people who are always late

- people who use other people

- irresponsible people

- certain songs

- going to church

- seeing young couples with children

- seeing people who smile all the time

- someone acting superior to me

- having to deal with new people

- thinking about my mistakes from the past

- being insulted with or without merit

- when people don't apologize for their mistakes

- when people don't do what they say they're going to do

- people who are opinionated and think that they're always right

- things that are too slow

- having financial trouble

- having no clothes

- being home all the time

- someone's death

- people that walk out on me

- having debt

- asking the same question over and over

- when someone doesn't discipline their child

- chewing gum loudly

- eating with a mouth open

- feeling invisible

- I want my space to be honored

- when people treat me out of "convenience" rather than genuine

- people who are cruel

- when people put me down

- people who gossip

- people who talk about their money

- being in a crowd

- waiting in line

- having too much work and not knowing where to start

- fixing other people mistakes

- going places I don't want to go

- people coming over without any notice

- sleep deprivation

- any kind of confrontation

- someone not listening to me

- people who have no goals

- not being organized

- certain names

- certain fragrances

The moment we are triggered our machine immediately covers up our vulnerability with a protection (coping mechanism) to keep our authentic safe. It interprets what the danger is and analyzes why. It does this so it can continue to justify its' belief system about the perceived dangers it's convinced are out there. Here are some examples of coping mechanisms the machine has to protect us. Remember, the coping behavior happens immediately along with a trigger so there is continuous protection.

- laughing
- being quiet
- screaming in a closet
- avoiding certain people
- watching funny movies
- listening to music
- smoking (pot, cigarettes)
- using illegal drugs
- watching TV
- masturbating
- excessive sex
- feeling numb
- take prescription meds
- becoming a stoic
- working out
- sleeping more
- eating more
- become verbally/physically abusive
- shopping
- crying
- self pity
- working more

- forced laughter

- staying busy/distracted

- becoming distant/isolating

- avoidance of people

- escaping into video games, books, TV, movies

- listening to music

- biting nails

- chewing the inside of mouth

- restless legs

- humming

- whistling

- running

- going to the park

- arguing

- keep asking questions

- saying mean, hurtful things

- not eating

- going for a drive

- sighing – taking deep breaths

- trying to stay busy

- going to church

- helping my mom

- drinking alcohol

- taking a hot shower

- praying

- laying on the couch

These coping mechanisms occur instantaneously with the trigger. In a nano second, quicker than a blink of your eye, we get triggered and are automatically defended – we don't have to think of anything. Our machine does this for us and we let it. We never question it until something happens that brings us to our knees: a heart attack, severe loss, frightening medical diagnosis, discovery of an affair, etc. Just like the tragedies I listed earlier, if the pain is extreme, our machines can't use the automatic coping mechanisms it has always relied on. They don't work because the pain is too great. Now, we have our closet door cracked open, with our prior pain and anger leaking out. The machine searches for immediate relief desperately batting down the hatches with full force.

HELLO TOM

There is an incredible story that I would like to share with you that has proven to be a significant lesson in my life. It is a very real demonstration of the power of the model that I have introduced in this book, and it begins with a situation that is very close to home. A few years ago, my wife and I put on a rather extensive second story and master bedroom addition to our home. During the course of this construction, my next door neighbor, Tom, was beginning to become irritated over what he perceived to believe to be an infringement of his privacy because of the construction and the placement of the windows as they faced the side of his property. Now, certainly all of this construction was done according to code and was approved by the city. However, Tom was beginning to show signs of agitation. I must tell you at this point that I live in a wonderfully sedate and safe neighborhood where many of our neighbors interact on a regular basis. In fact, the neighbor on the other side of me has put in a fence with a gate in between so our children could walk back and forth as they shared different experiences and played together. Tom is an angry and divorced man, and had visitation of his two sons. He rarely interacted with the other neighbors, always keeping to himself.

One day I was driving home and I waved to Tom and as usual he did not wave to me. Rather, he turned his car around, parked it and began yelling at me about the addition. He was pointing his finger at me and, using the vernacular in this book, was triggered, in a massive way. His yelling began to escalate and I was becoming extremely self-conscious because I was with my children at the time and they were beginning to get worried and uncomfortable. I immediately got out of the vehicle and began to try to show some kind of understanding and compassion for what he was trying to say about the addition, the window, and the like. I invited him to go on his property so that we might take a closer look at what was obviously bothering him a great deal. As I was walking up the driveway I remember feeling a tremendous degree of anxiety and fear and was indeed triggered myself. I was clearly remembering childhood experiences where I was picked on by many of the bullies and, in some ways, Tom's considerable size and "crazy looking eyes" was making me feel like I was back in the seventh grade and being intimidated once again. The only thing I could think of doing at the time was to try to remain "Dr. French" and begin to treat this massive triggering by Tom as a clinical intervention with a patient who was escalating. I was somewhat successful at doing this by trying to hear Tom's anger and not respond defensively to it. He began making references about my wife, Cindy, and it was beginning to get even more intense. After a considerable amount of time, which felt more like two hours, which was apparently only twenty minutes, he went into his house still hot under the collar but at least feeling like he had let me have a piece of his mind (machine).

I went home and told Cindy about it and we both tried to let the situation go and continue on with our life. A couple of days later she called me at work and indicated that he was glaring at her while she walked the children to school. I asked what she meant by glaring and she made a very vivid description of how he continued to stare at her with this intimidating gaze that even made the other neighbors who walk to school with my wife uncomfortable. The next morning we awoke to the sound of Tom hammering away and sawing, only to discover that he was putting up a large and long fence between our properties. In fact, he ran the fence all the way down to the curb. I went out to try to talk to him and he just glared at me. I was again triggered and knew that I was becoming increasingly more uncomfortable with the situation that was starting to look like it was getting out of control. Believe it or not it did continue to get out of control. He took a large white door and spray painted on it "Stress Center" with a big red arrow pointing at our house and put it on top of his garage! Cindy called me again, so when I drove home I passed by Tom's house to see this large door on top of his garage, almost like a billboard, with an arrow pointing to our home. I would also add that the sign in front of my office at that time was a sign with the words "Stress Center." We went upstairs and closed the windows so we would not have to look at it. So, Tom's method of intimidation and getting us to close the blinds was quite effective. If we left them open we were continuing to see this eye sore which appeared right outside of reach of our window, and if we closed the blinds we could not enjoy the light that was coming through the windows. Obviously, Tom, in his paranoia, thought that we were going to peek down or gaze down into the windows to look at him or observe him, when we had no intention of doing anything like that. We merely wanted this type of window in our master bedroom to let in light. A few days later we noticed that Tom had gone to the trouble of putting two or three flood lights in place of his porch light which shone very intensely and strategically into our bedroom. Of course, in the evening it lit up our entire bedroom so it was almost like daylight. We had difficulty sleeping and I found myself triggered, distressed, uncomfortable, and getting angrier by the moment. I continued to receive reports from Cindy that he was glaring and gazing at her and the children as they walked to school, so I began to seek out some advice from others in the neighborhood. My one next door neighbor on the other side is a Whittier police office and he felt there wasn't much we could do and that Tom had not really broken any laws so what we might try to do is see if we could diffuse the situation by just waiting. I agreed and spoke with some of the other neighbors all of whom were to some degree, intimidated. However, Tom was not glaring at them; he was glaring at *my family*.

The next day something even more incredible happened. Tom turned the door around and spray painted a new sign which read *"GOT ANY PRIVACY?"* and put that back in its' original state on top of his garage. He accompanied this sign with another smaller sign in his kitchen window which said *"ENJOY IT WHILE YOU CAN."*

Now it was clearly out of hand. I pondered whether or not this was indeed a real threat, or one which I could take legal action, or one which I should take personally as a threat to my family or to me. I then did the next thing that I knew to do, which was to call the police chief who was a personal friend. I was the Police Psychologist for the City of Whittier in addition to a number of other cities, so I felt that I could ask his advice directly. After hearing the situation he showed a lot of sensitivity and compassion and said basically that I had to "remain the victim." The sign that indicated *"ENJOY IT WHILE YOU CAN"* was in a "gray area" of interpretation as to whether or not it was a real threat.

So, here I was once again uncomfortable with what to do and feeling more and more helpless, in what I believed to be a genuine threat. In the meantime, we had called the city and found out about the fence. We discovered that it was illegal to build a fence all the way down the curb. So, a representative from the city ended up going to Tom's house and you might expect what Tom's reaction was when he was informed that he must cut the fence back from the curb several feet. Talk about massively triggered! He went about cutting his fence without taking it down. He merely took a skill saw and went right along the fence. He then took fish line and constructed it in such a way to that his ivy would grow into the fish line and form a new barrier which would replace the fence he had cut down. All of this was indeed getting more and more complicated, and I was getting more and more uncomfortable. The flood light situation only lasted two or three days. So, he apparently changed the lighting back to the porch light, but he did leave that on all night long. On occasion, he would play certain music or a sports station at various times, at just enough of an annoying level, but not yet one that would cause a disturbing the peace signal. I then went back to the police station and discussed the matter with them in more detail, and they advised me that I could seek a restraining order. However, it would only be temporary and might only last a few weeks.

One day my daughter Jennifer went out to play and came back in rather quickly and looked very frightened. I immediately asked her what was wrong and she said she didn't feel comfortable going out because "Tom was out there." Well, that was it for me. I immediately ran out went to the edge of my property, glared at him and was ready to do battle because I was massively triggered and was out of options. He was now threatening, or what I believed to be threatening my daughter, and he had crossed the line. His size and his massive machine triggering were not going to trigger me anymore. He represented all the bullies who had pinned me down and washed my face out with snow and thrown my glasses around in mockery and humiliation. I was ready to have some finality and closure and it didn't matter to me who was going to stand up and who was going to fall down, I wanted it over with. He saw my eyes and he must have felt and seen my intensity, because he turned away. I don't even know if that was a victory, but I felt like I had won some piece of my own dignity back and restored my sense of competency and security in regards to my family.

A few days later a squad car came to my house and the policeman indicated that a call had come in from my neighbor (obviously Tom), indicating that our van had been parked in front of our house for over a three day period and it needed to be moved or it would be towed away. He profoundly apologized, but said he was doing his job. I went out and moved the van around the block so that the speedometer reading would indicate that the van had been moved and wondered to myself if this was something Tom was going to do every two or three days just to agitate and harass me. I asked the policeman if he could please go over to Tom's house and request that Tom and I and the policeman have a discussion. I thought with the policeman present acting as an armed referee, I might have the opportunity to begin some dialogue and communication. The policeman returned saying that Tom was too angry and upset with my wife and I to have any conversation at this time. Now I found myself continually uncomfortable, coming home and even the mere sight of Tom's red car would act as a major trigger for me and once I was triggered the next behavior that I would exhibit in terms of my coping was to feel nauseated, helpless, fearful, anxious and uncomfortable. I didn't like being the victim, I didn't like playing the game, and

I felt helpless about anything that I could do about it. I kept seeking refuge inside trying to figure out what I must do and how I could get through this. It continued to remind me of that original pain of my childhood.

It was near the Fourth of July and our neighborhood decided to have a block party. My wife and I and a few other neighbors decided to host the event and it would be our first annual Fourth of July block party. We went to the city and found out that we must have signatures of at least two thirds of the neighbors in our area in order to host the block party and have the barriers put up by the city. Believe it or not, one of the neighbors who went around collecting signatures indicated that Tom signed the petition! I thought to myself, well now he's going to be there, but there will be enough people, yet I know I am going to be uncomfortable because just being around him or being near him was giving me a whole new definition of the word triggered.

It was about one week before the event, and I was mowing my lawn, I saw Tom jogging down the street, which he occasionally did. As I saw him jogging, I thought to myself "What would Christ do right now?" And I answered myself with "He would love him, He would forgive him." Just as I had that thought, Tom stopped running and started walking up his driveway after completing his route. I shut the lawn mower off, went to the edge of my property, took a deep breath, and slowly and softly said "Hello Tom." He glared at me, and made the most disgusting, repulsive face that I have seen since I was a child, and he stomped into his house mumbling under his breath. Obviously this made me very uncomfortable and I remember gulping at the time and sighing very heavily. I continued to do the work on my lawn all the time wondering what I was going to do about the Fourth of July and how I was going to deal with this problem that seemed to have no end. Well, the week passed and it was the day before the Fourth of July and I was now at the bottom of my property doing some weeding with my next door neighbor, Mike, the police officer, who was helping me (we occasionally would help each other). As we were working together, I saw Tom's red car, which of course triggered me and he started to drive up his driveway but stopped, screeching his brakes, of course, and he flung his door open and got out of his car. Now you've got to picture the scene: I am on my knees pulling weeds, and I looked up and I was somewhat blinded by the sun, I saw Tom's six foot something frame hovering over me hands on his hips and I believed that this was the moment of truth. My next thought was, well, I have the weeder in my right hand and I have the cop on the other side. Let's get it over with because my machine clearly perceived this to be a dangerous situation because

Tom had now crossed the line. I stood up somewhat reluctantly and apprehensively. Tom looked at me and said, "Hi Dave" and extended his right hand. I immediately said, "Tom, do you mean this?" He said, "Yes" and we shook hands. He then said, "Dave, I've been a jerk and I want you to know that you and your wife have never done anything to really hurt me, and you are good people, but I've been smoking a lot of weed and my mind has been getting messed up ever since my divorce and I've acted like a fool, but I want you to know that when you said hello to me the other day while I was running, I went in the house and felt terrible. I remember changing my clothes and I felt disgusted and knew that you were being very kind to me. So, I want to know if you can find it in your heart, would you forgive me." I was so overwhelmed and so relieved that I said excitedly, "Yes, I'll forgive you." We both hugged each other and cried. Tom was crying, I was crying, we were both laughing and believe me, the policeman almost dropped his weeder and his jaw was wide open. There we stood hugging and laughing. Mike the policeman left and Tom and I continued to chat and spend the next couple of hours together. I talked to him about my work, my life, and the first book I had written. He asked for a copy of it and I gave it to him. The next day we were at the Fourth of July party standing side by side barbequing a couple hundred hamburgers! The moral of the story for me was to _treat people better than they deserve._ Show mercy, and mercy to me is showing _undeserved forgiveness._ You won't believe this, it even gets better. While Tom and I were making hamburgers, he said to me, "You know Dave, that fence I build needs to come down, how about you and I taking it down soon?" I said, "Sure, Tom." So, there I was the following day, 6:00 a.m., in Tom's home. He's making me coffee and waffles, while we're chatting, we go outside and he says, "You get the first swing," and he hands me a large sledgehammer. Of course, I take out four boards at once with the first swipe. "It feels good," Tom laughs. Then he says something extremely profound, "You know Dave, my machine built this fence out of anger and now you and I are taking it down out of love!" I dropped the hammer, I cried, we hugged each other again. The entire fence comes down. We stack the wood together and pick up the nails and continue to share philosophically about life in terms of the model and the work that I'm doing. Tom is fascinated by this model and now has a very clear understanding of what has happened to him and he says to me, "You must have really hated my machine" and I said, "Yeah, I really did, Tom." In fact, I ended up sharing with him many of the fantasies I had, and some of the feelings that I had about his machine and some of the things I'd wanted to do like, shoot the flood light with a b.b. gun, burn the fence down, etc., etc. We both laughed and then he said "Dave, I'm a little embarrassed to tell you this, but come over here and take a look." I walked over to a section of his driveway and he showed me some large holes that had been filled up with concrete. He remarked, "You know Dave, my machine was so out of control that I went down to the city and got approval for plans to build a fifteen foot carport fence." He then said, "After I had the holds dug, I realized I was out of control and had to fill them up. That's how bad it got." We continued to meet, Tom later apologized to my wife Cindy and he now has become a brother and friend. He flattered me with saying I was the "Babe Ruth of Psychology." Tom had run a baseball card shop and he gave me a rare photograph of Babe Ruth with his wife and daughter. On the back he inscribed, "To my brother, Dave, thanks for the home run, your brother, Tom." He brought us avocados from his tree on Thanksgiving. We exchanged Christmas presents that year and I wanted to ask him to serve on a committee for my nonprofit Foundation for Personal Balance. Miracles can happen if you live authentically and trust in God and in yourself. Is this a story or what?

Recently, I had asked Tom if he would like to share his perspective regarding the incident and have it included in this book. He was very excited about the opportunity to share his feelings. The following account is in Tom's own words: "I didn't understand the struggle that was going on inside me. All I knew is I was angry; angry with my neighbors, my ex-wife, and myself. I knew it was wrong, but couldn't overcome it. A battle was raging inside of me and it was tearing me apart. The only people I could truly show love to were my sons. I always knew how much love my heart held and the depth of intimacy I am capable of, but I could not understand why I was so afraid to show it; to trust, to let it out. I felt tired, and the anger carried with me was a load that was dragging me down. I had built a wall around my heart – the one my mother had torn apart for years in her alcoholic rages. I had taken the last little piece and put it away, so deep, so far inside of me that no one could possibly ever hurt me again. I had to survive, to make it.

I had made myself a promise that when I had children, I was going to give them a happy home free from the terror, the horror I knew as a child, but there was no sanctuary at home. Imagine if you will, coming home after a day of work to relax at home in a wonderful neighborhood full of children only to remember when I pulled in my driveway that I was angry with my neighbors. The people behind my house had built on their addition had invaded my privacy. I didn't like it. Then Dave French built on to his house next door. The second story addition that had windows that looked into my backyard. I let it get to me. I let it bother me. Then Mike and Suzy (neighbors on this other side) messed up my wall on the other side of me. I got angry about that and let it destroy our friendship. The machine I had built to protect myself to run my life grew stronger with each bolt of anger and hatred it took to assemble it. I had even built a fence between Dave's and my house. I knew it was wrong; built out of anger; but I did it anyway. I built it just like I had built the wall around my heart, but now this machine was destroying my life. It took from me the most important thing that we give to others, love! It stopped me from trusting, it stopped me from being me, from being real. Why couldn't I love my neighbor, why couldn't I love my girlfriend, why couldn't I trust myself, why couldn't I let my love out?

The first shot was fired. My girlfriend said good-bye, I was wounded. She had watched me love my sons, but I couldn't let my love out for her, I couldn't trust. The bullet got through the layers of armor but I was able to function, to shake it off and go on.

And then the second shot, the one that finished me off was fired by Dave French.

I had gone for a run to relax, to forget about my girlfriend. Then I come back home and there was Dave on the corner of his lawn right next to my driveway. I saw him as I came down the street and thought "great, just what I need." I knew he wasn't a bad guy and had to keep reminding myself why I didn't like him. As I began walking up the driveway, I heard him say "Hello Tom," I mumbled, "Yeah, Hi Dave" and went ahead to my house. That "Hello Tom" got through. It bounced around inside and I felt it. I felt the warmth of a human being reaching out to me. I felt the forgiveness from a man who owed me nothing. I felt his love. I felt me.

Well, the Fourth of July was just a few days away and the whole street was going to have a block party. I didn't know how I was going to do it. To go outside and be with my neighbors, I was worried. Then it happened, a moment I will always remember, one that would change my life so dramatically that I would never be the same.

I was coming home after running some errands driving up the street, who did I see at the driveway pulling some weeds, getting ready for the big party? Yes, it was Dave French. I pulled in and got out of my car. I remember looking at the kitchen door of my house and then at Dave. Each was an equal distance away, maybe 30 feet or so. I looked again at the door and then at Dave. It was at that point I knew I had a decision to make. Go back inside or go towards Dave. I was scared to death, but I also felt strength. God was there. I felt him help me with his gentle loving hand; pushing me toward my neighbor, Dave. I was on my way. I remember Dave looking up at me as he heard my footsteps approaching. I vividly remember seeing the puzzled look in his eyes. "What is Tom doing?" it said "What is going on?" It was at that point I held out my open hand and said, "I'm sorry Dave, I'm sorry." He stood up and I could see the feelings that were going through him through his eyes... The power of the moment was nothing short of spiritual, it was of God. Dave murmured "Oh my God" and began to cry. I was trembling, but not from fear. It was from letting go. We hugged each other and I felt the love in me, the love for my neighbor, I was real. I had done it, it was over, but I had just begun. I don't remember how long we talked, but it was a long time. I opened my heart and Dave accepted. Something wonderful had happened and I felt good.

Dave had explained the "machine" I built to protect myself, and my real self. I have read his first book. The more I read, the more I saw of myself and the more sense it made to me. I began to clearly see the struggle that had taken place in me for many years. I was on my way to being real and to stopping this machine that had been running my life. I was on my way to loving, to feeling, to being me. Dave was right there all the time, right under my nose.

It was time for the fence to come down. The one I had built between our houses. We agreed that the following Saturday at 6:00 a.m., we would take it down together. As we worked side by side that morning, I saw meaning in our task. I watched as each swing of our hammers removed the boards which were pounded into place with nails of hatred. Our hammers were removing those nails. It is the same way the "machine" is built, with anger and hatred. The way that it is taken apart is with "love."

"Thanks Dave, I love you!"

ANXIETY AND DEPRESSION

Are you anxious or are you depressed? What is depression? Depression is not what you might think it is. The way we have defined it or the way that it appears is an individual who is moping, sad, looking down, and very, very uncomfortable. Let me remind you of the Winnie the Pooh series. All the characters are very representative and symbolic of many facets of the human personality. Eeyore has a rain cloud constantly over his head and has an attitude of despair, hopelessness, and a constant preoccupation of his tail falling off. Winnie the Pooh is a soft and tender authentic bear who represents our authentic self. Tigger is the rambunctious teenager full of animation and passion who is constantly on hyper-drive as he races through life bouncing off his tail only intermittently interacting with the other characters. The rabbit is neurotic because he is obsessed with his garden. The little pig stutters because he's insecure and frightened. The owl is very intellectual and analytical, never showing or displaying any genuine emotion, sounding more like a computer offering his intellect for guidance. Out of some of the characters just mentioned, it may surprise you to know that the one that is truly depressed would not be Eeyore, but would in fact be the owl. Let me explain what this means and why I've chosen the owl to be a representative of what depression really is. Imagine a Kleenex box. The tissue in its' many layers is soft and fragile and delicate and represents our pain. The hard box represents our anger. The anger covers up the softer more vulnerable tissue. The anger is a defensive layer against the vulnerable tenderness and fragility of our pain. The two travel together. Whenever you see a person angry, it's because right under the surface they are hurt. So the tissue box becomes a very simple, yet powerful representation of how feelings are packaged inside of us. Since the machine avoids pain and seeks out pleasure, it can't handle feeling the anger, because you can't walk around angry all day, and it can't handle expressing any pain because of how vulnerable that feels, so what the machine does is it stores the anger and the pain in the tissue box inside of a closet. God gives us enough space inside, one conventional closet that we are issued at birth, to store things in. Over time, people continue to store lots of tissue and lots of boxes in order to protect themselves from feeling the vulnerability and helplessness of their pain. Now imagine further, that this closet door is shut. The closet door is a defense that protects the person from feeling the anger and the pain that's inside the closet. Imagine this closet to be a junk closet; stuffed completely full of all kinds of feelings, all kinds of anger, and all kinds of trauma that has been experienced. The closet door remains shut, and imagine that the machine has to keep the pressure on holding that closet closed. The word emotion is an interesting word and I am going to give you a different way of looking at it. If you remove the "e" from the word emotion; "e" stands for energy, energy in motion is an emotion. There is an energy to these feelings and to this anger, there is a charge to it, and of course, it takes energy by the machine, to keep the closet door shut so that we can function in our daily lives and we can continue to survive. It takes a lot of energy, your energy, to keep the door closed. Now, at this point, the mind can't open the door because it's afraid that if it opens the door and all the junk falls out of it, like a lava flow of emotions and anger; it would be overwhelmed. In fact, the mind views this as a loss of control, or even insanity, so it will refuse to open that door because it's now way too full. The feelings on the inside want to come out. The mind needs to hold them in, so there's a constant pressure which results in fatigue. A person who is depressed feels the following things:

Fatigue (the energy it takes to keep the closet door shut and the feelings in)

Loss of concentration

Difficulty concentrating

A loss of motivation

A loss of joy (Anhedonia)

A loss of libido (sex drive)

Interrupted sleep

Early morning awakening

Difficulty falling asleep (the machine continually thinking)

Weight gain or weight loss

Loss of appetite (some people eat too much; others can't eat at all)

Some people can sleep to cope with the pain; others can't easily fall asleep

We have a lighthearted expression; we say that if all of our depressed patients called each other at three o'clock in the morning, they'd all be awake! Three o'clock seems to be the magic time that depressed people wake up in the middle of the night.

The reason is simple. As mentioned earlier, the emotions that are stored inside want to come out and be expressed. The mind, in its' effort to survive, needs to keep them held shut. The constant pressure is there when someone is trying to fall asleep. Depressed people have difficulty falling asleep because their mind is racing and it's trying to figure out and analyze what happened during that day, what might happen tomorrow, what could happen, etc. So, imagine if you will, the person is trying to fall asleep while they are holding one hand on that closet door inside of themselves to keep the emotions in check. When they fall asleep out of exhaustion their ability to keep the closet door shut is compromised because of the sleeping state. What happens after a few hours is the feelings now start to come out because the guard of the door is no longer pressing against it to keep it closed. Then what happens is people wake up. That is what's waking a depressed person up in the middle of the night; it's the loss on control over holding the feelings in and the potential of the feelings coming out on their own awakens the person from a sleep only to get back into control again. Once the person has restored its' control after a half an hour or an hour, they are able to try to fall back to sleep again. Now imagine that this internal pressure that's created from all those harbored feelings becomes more intense. When it becomes that intense, imagine the door shaking or rumbling from the internal pressure. This rumbling or shaking is what's known as anxiety. Anxiety is a result of the internal pressure of all the harbored anger and feelings that are held inside. It is very similar to an aftershock of an earthquake. Those rumblings represent the pressure resulting from the internal pressure. A person could be looking at the cantaloupes at a market, and all of a sudden start to feel a wave of panic, or a wave of anxiety and tearfulness. The cantaloupe aren't causing that reaction, it is just that at that moment in time, the emotions demand to be expressed and released. Their mind/their machine, is stopping those feelings from coming out, because the person is fearful of a great loss of control, so a panic attack results. The person could even be doing something at a moment in time that's quite relaxing; maybe they are gathered with friends and interacting and socializing, all of a sudden, that wave of anxiety hits and they are now in a compromised state feeling the excessive sensation of restlessness and fearfulness and they do not know why. At that moment, the mind is trying to figure out why they would have this anxiety during this peaceful time, and that's because the repressed emotions have now built up enough pressure so that they demand immediate release. The persons' machine continues to press the door closed, keep the door shut, and the result is a wave of anxiety that overtakes them and can result in a very helpless feeling of panic.

So, to summarize, we have one conventional closet; with only so much psychic space to be used. We have a lot of anger which is the next layer below the closet door and we have a lot of pain and hurt that the anger is masking. There are other assorted pieces in there from other traumas in our life, so it's very important to know that in this metaphor, it is indeed the closet door that is the depression. Depression is like emotional novocaine. The numbing sensation that you experience at the dentist's office is a similar kind of numbing on the psyche in order for depression to occur. The closet door is the numbing and it's defending or masking against the two emotions that are inside which is a lot of anger and a lot of pain. The build-up of the internalization of these two emotions, is what causes that internal pressure, as mentioned earlier, which is anxiety. Pressure results from a rattling of the closet door, which the person experiences as intermittent anxiety or acute anxiety, or a panic attack. Remember again, the mind is in the business of controlling and in the business of protecting us. It will not turn around and open that closet door for fear that the lava flow of emotions will overwhelm it, because it will experience its' greatest fear, which is the loss of self, or insanity. (Ego death).

Little children release their feelings immediately and they do so in real time and remain pretty much in the present mode. As mentioned earlier, around eight or ten years of age, as we are socializing and wanting to be liked and loved, the machine appears in a more dramatic form as the formation of the mask hiding our true identity. We learn the automatic smile, and the automatic laughter. We learn how to have certain intonations in our voice that will allow people to think that we're feeling something else, or try to get people to believe that we're feeling other things other than what we really are. The mask, or the layer of the machine protection, is the beginning of the road that can lead to mild, moderate, or severe depression. If we continue to hide feelings and mask those feelings of pain and anger, we continue to utilize the armored numbness of the closet door, and we are on our way to becoming more depressed. Remember, depression takes a lot of energy, the energy from the internalized feelings is held in check by the energy of the machine trying to keep the closet door shut. It would be like two hands pressing against each other, both exerting a lot of force. That expenditure of energy, in order to just "survive" is why depressed people have a tremendous amount of fatigue. There is also anxiety that results from the machines' extraordinary anticipation of the future. As mentioned earlier, the machine, in driving the car through life, uses binoculars in order to anticipate and second guess what might happen, could happen, for certain will happen, is likely to happen, and so on. This future thinking fueled by our fear and uncertainty, feeds another layer of anxiety. So there is anxiety that exists from the internal pressure, and anxiety that exists in the automatic thinking of the mind trying to anticipate all forms of danger, so as to protect its' most prized possession and jewel, the authentic. There are a number of treatments for depression, and the ones that work best also combat anxiety. Cognitive behavioral therapy gets at response patterns central to both conditions. The drugs most commonly used in treating depression are: SSRI's (Selective Serotonin Reuptake Inhibitors), and they have also been proven effective against an array of anxiety disorders from social phobia to panic and post traumatic stress. Depression is one of the most common psychological problems affecting nearly everyone through either personal experience, or even through depression in a family member. Each year over seventeen million American adults experience a period of clinical depression. Depression can interfere with normal functioning, frequently causing problems with work, social, and family life.

There are three main types of depressive disorders: Major depression, Dysthymia, and Bipolar Disorder. They can occur with any of the anxiety disorders. Major depression involves at least five symptoms listed previously for a two week period. Such an episode is disabling and will interfere with the ability to work, study, eat, and sleep, as mentioned earlier. Major depressive episodes can occur once or twice in a lifetime, and they may reoccur frequently. They may also take place spontaneously during or after the death of a loved one, a romantic break up, medical illness, or another life event. Some people with major depression may feel that life is not worth living, and some will even attempt to end their lives. Dysthymia is a less severe, long term and chronic form of depression. It involves the same symptoms of major depression, as mentioned earlier, mainly low energy, poor appetite, or overeating, and insomnia, or oversleeping, it can manifest itself as stress, irritability, and mild anhedonia, which is the inability to derive pleasure from most activities or activities that one truly enjoyed. People with dysthymia might be thought of as always seeing the glass as half empty. Bipolar disorder, (which used to be called manic depression), is characterized by a mood cycle that shifts from severe highs (known as mania), or mild highs (hypo-mania), to severe lows (depression). During a manic phase, the person may experience abnormal or excessive elation. Excessive elation, irritability, or a decreased need for sleep, grandiose notions, increased talking, racing thoughts,

increased sexual desire, marked increased energy, poor judgment, inappropriate social behavior, gambling sprees, shopping sprees, etc. During the depressive phase, a
person experiences the same symptoms, as one would suffering from major depression. Mood swings from manic to depressive are often gradual, although occasionally they can occur abruptly.

Some symptoms of anxiety will include: feelings of apprehension or dread,
trouble concentrating, feeling tense and jumpy, anticipating the worst, irritability,
restlessness, watching for signs of danger, feeling like your mind has gone blank.
There are also common physical symptoms of anxiety that include: pounding heart,
sweating, stomach upset, or dizziness, frequent urination or diarrhea, shortness of
breath, tremors and twitches, muscle tension, headaches, fatigue, and insomnia. The
symptoms of a anxiety attack include: Surge of overwhelming panic, feeling you are
losing control or going crazy, heart palpitations or chest pain, feeling like you are going to pass out, trouble breathing or choking sensation, feeling like the room is clos-
ing in on you, hyperventilation, hot flashes or chills, trembling or shaking, nausea or
stomach cramps, feeling detached or unreal. There are six types of anxiety disorders
each with their own distinct symptoms, they are: Generalized Anxiety Disorder, Ob-
sessive/Compulsive Disorder, Panic Disorder, Phobia, Post Traumatic Stress Disorder, and Social Anxiety Disorder. In a generalized anxiety disorder there are constant
worries and fears that distract a person from their day to day activities. They are filled
with impending doom, like something very bad is going to happen. In obsessive
compulsive disorder, there are unwanted thoughts or behaviors that seem impossible to stop or control. If you have OCD, you may be troubled by obsessions such
as a reoccurring worry that you forgot to turn off the oven, or that you might hurt
someone. This is the machine in a very highly charged state. The panic disorder is
characterized by repeated, unexpected panic attacks as well as fear of experiencing
another episode. Panic Disorder may also be accompanied by agoraphobia which
is a fear of being in places where escape of help would be difficult in the event of a
panic attack. If you have agoraphobia you are likely to avoid public places such as
shopping malls, or confined spaces, such as an airplane. A phobia is an unrealistic or
exaggerated fear of a specific object, activity, or situation that in reality presents little
or no danger. Common phobias include fear of animals, such as snakes and spiders,
fear of flying, and fear of heights. In the case of severe phobia you might go to extreme lengths to avoid the thing you fear, unfortunately, avoidance only strengthens

and feeds the phobia. Post Traumatic Stress Disorder (PTSD), is an anxiety disorder that can occur in the aftermath of a traumatic or life threatening event. Symptoms of PTSD include, flashbacks or nightmares about what happened, hyper-vigilance, startling easily, withdrawing from others, and avoiding situations that remind you of the event. If you have a debilitating fear of being seen negatively by others and humiliated in public, you may have Social Anxiety Disorder which is also known as Social Phobia. Social Anxiety Disorder can be thought of as extreme shyness. In severe cases, social situations are avoided all together. Performance Anxiety (better known as stage fright) is the most common type of social phobia.

This chapter has focused on anxiety and depression and I've used my simple metaphor of the closet to describe what the mind does with its' pain in an effort to avoid feeling overwhelmed. In its' mission to protect us it uses the closet to store all unwanted feelings and tries to forget what happened because it is spending most of its' time surviving life, rather than living it. As mentioned earlier, its' using the binoculars to look into the future, and the rear view mirror to remember the past so that it's constantly trying to anticipate ways to protect us from perceived danger. When the machine cannot perform its' mission and give us the protection that we need because the conventional things that it's using aren't working anymore, the machine has to resort to another measure. If storing the feelings in the closet doesn't work because of the numbness that it uses to remove us from the feeling or maybe the alcohol that it drinks that also numbs us no longer has the effect of helping us forget, or maybe the drugs that we use, or the pot that we smoke no longer gives us distance from the pain, the machine has to resort to its' ultimate form of protection, suicide. Yes, I use the word protection in regards to suicide. Suicide is the ultimate form of protection by the mind. Remember, the minds mission is to protect us above all else. If the standard forms and conventional measures it uses do not work, the machine actually views suicide as a way of stopping the pain. It is not thinking about killing itself, it's not even thinking about tomorrow. It's thinking about *stopping the pain.* That is why many people will say, she was a straight A student, how could she kill herself, or the man had everything going for him, a wonderful wife, children, he went to church regularly, what happened to him. It's very difficult for people to understand why the mind would commit this act.

Years ago, I had a patient who was in Vietnam and he was part of the Mi Lai massacre. During this particular massacre, soldiers who had previously been taunted by the Vietcong by seeing the heads of their fellow soldiers on stakes entered a village feeling a lot of rage and wanting to unload that rage on whoever was there. The massacre occurred. My patient remembered seeing a couple of mothers going near the river as this was going on and slowly submerging their babies under the water. He was horrified by this act. My interpretation of this was that these mothers were anticipating a violent death for themselves and their babies. By slowly submerging them with the gentleness of their touch under the water, these babies were put out of their misery and were prevented from feeling a violent ending. This is very much like the machine, in doing its' ultimate protection of suicide. Suicide is a gentle submerging of slowly putting the authentic in a quiet, peaceful state so that it will not have to feel the pain of the impending doom that the mind is convinced is there. That is why before a suicide, many patients will look peaceful and at ease. They will look rested and assured, confident. That is why they will come by to say thank you, or goodbye. Remember, out of one hundred thousand people who say they want to kill themselves, only about ten actually do. I've looked at suicide in three different levels: there is ideation, there is a gesture, and there is what I call the attempt. "Ideation" means that the machine is anticipating or thinking impulsively about thoughts of suicide, one might say, I wonder what would happen if I turn my steering wheel to the left and drove into oncoming traffic right now, or someone might say, I'm just a couple of feet away from the edge of this cliff while driving in the mountains, I wonder what would happen if I turned and went over. These impulsive thoughts are just a way to release a sort of psychic pressure so it can momentarily get rid of a peak amount of pain or fear that might be experienced at that moment. A "gesture" is where someone might ingest several valium and drink a pint of rum and then call one of their friends immediately to say what they've just done. Of course, the friend will call the paramedics and the person will get to the hospital, have their stomach pumped and will of course survive. The attempt is a much more serious matter. This is where the machine methodically plans out how it's going to remove itself and its' precious jewel from all the pain that it's experiencing. This is the plan to comfort the jewel of the authentic. It's the ultimate form of protection so that the machine can fulfill *its' mission* of standing guard with its' most prized possession, us.

PAIN

Many machines are narcissistic and are "driven." We often use the term "driven" to describe someone who's successful as we say "isn't she driven" or "they are so driven" and how true that is. Unfortunately, what is driving them is their machine. In the middle of all this narcissistic drive for greed and power and the incredible advances we have made technologically we find that the gift of the authentic self is a closely kept secret. We make quiet connections with those we're safe with and we value the words of children, we look to the minister for the word of God and to the printed word in the Bible. We are always touched when we hear the voice of the authentic and we are moved when we see the gift of the authentic represented in painting, music, drama or the like. We have become somewhat hedonistic in our pursuit of life. The machine is driven to survive and cope and by what other machines' definitions of success are. We have lost control of ourselves and it is clearly reflected in the tremendous turbulence that we see today in our streets, cities and communities. There are many dysfunctional people walking the streets and there are inadequate facilities to care for them.

In this driven quest the machine is operating in its' basic search for pleasure and avoidance of pain. We are taught that pain is bad, that pleasure is good or certainly the absence of pain is good. We are uncomfortable when someone else is feeling pain. This is certainly true of many couples I have seen in psychotherapy for marital counseling. Typically the woman is feeling pain and the man is uncomfortable with her expression of it. The metaphor I use is that when a woman is feeling pain it is like she is in the water and thrashing about. Men who are driven in a rational and concrete way, want to throw ropes and rafts in the water and attempt to rescue the woman. What the woman truly wants is for the man to get in the water with her and **_be with her and her pain._**

Unfortunately, this makes a demand on the man to experience the same **_level_** of pain that the woman is experiencing. In other words, when a person is feeling pain they are experiencing it and in order to connect with them one must go to that same level within themselves. When this is accomplished one is now aware of what is hurting them at that level and it causes them discomfort. So, going to that level is essentially a trigger. One is triggered because one perceives going to that level as threatening. So, therefore the man has difficulty joining the woman emotionally at the level she needs him because the man believes he must "make the woman okay." So, in his concrete way he tries to help her feel better and avoid the pain.

Pain that you feel is *your* pain and since it is your pain it must be experienced by you so to deny or avoid it is to deny your own authenticity and real self. Many times I ask my patients "If you weren't coping right now and if you weren't thinking right now what would you be feeling?" Many times most of us are coping, surviving, thinking, analyzing, rationalizing, defending, distracting, denying and doing everything but *feeling* what if is that we're afraid of or uncomfortable with. What has happened is that our machine frames feeling our pain as dangerous and therefore it is triggered not to want to respond to it and proceeds to protect us. Imagine what we're doing to ourselves. The machine is programmed to help us survive and we have some discomfort or pain (let's call it helplessness). We need to feel the helplessness in order to process the helplessness, but as we begin to feel it we are triggered because the machine perceives feeling the helplessness as a loss of control and that, of course, is perceived as threatening and dangerous because we might go crazy or melt or God knows what. So since the machine does not know what we'll do if we let ourselves feel this helplessness and we don't have any "guarantee," then it does the next conservative thing. ***It decides it must be dangerous*** or it might be dangerous and therefore is dangerous. We are triggered and therefore we are protected and we remain helpless (this time our helplessness is now repressed). We function with our persona and public face of smiling and talking and jabbering and jabbering when in fact, we are denying what is truly there. Now, you might wonder what person would want to feel that helplessness and why would someone want to feel that pain? Well, the answer is quite simple ***because it is your pain*** . It's not my pain, it's not Jim's pain, it's not Linda's pain, it's your pain. And because it is your pain it is your responsibility to express it.

I had mentioned in my previous book a very interesting notion and that is if someone was laughing hysterically aren't you delighted by their amusement and joy? Don't you want to encourage them to laugh more? Does it not delight you to see them happy and having pleasure? Why then can't we be encouraged to feel our pain? Why can't we celebrate our sadness? Why can't we be encouraged to go into the darkness? I have called this place of pain for myself the "black forest." The black forest is that place inside of me where I go to feel many minutes and hours of hurt, helplessness, and pain. It is the place where I am afraid, confused, lonely, scared, doubting, wondering, worrying and on occasion have felt despair. It is a place where I want to believe, but have trouble believing and where it would sure be nice to have mom and dad there to take care of me, but they are not there to take care of me. It is my own private place of pain and each time I go there and sit there and surrender to the experience I feel peace and serenity and actually, a "sweetness" in the mist of the jungle of pain. Please try to understand what I am saying at this point. I'm saying that you must embrace your pain with the same degree of passion and fervor that you would embrace your pleasure. Once you experience the pain of helplessness, for example, the machine will no longer be triggered because it sees that **_you go there and you return_**. The "returning" is essential in order to modify the machine because it gets strengthened and continues to justify its' existence if it proves it's prophecy to be true. One has to educate one's machine. One has to risk in areas where the machine, acting like a critical parent, is warning you not to go. You must go on your own accord, risk the insanity and emotional death, come back and report to the machine that you are unharmed. Once the machine can witness that you are indeed alright, you can make a modification in its hard wiring and its programming. The modification will help prevent you from being triggered in the future. Thus, "the work" is to become aware of the moment you are triggered. As you begin to go into another behavior, which will allow you to cope and survive the perceived pain, you can stop yourself from going into that place by **_making the choice_** to surrender to the pain that the machine is hiding from. You can go through the pain by logging some real time in the black forest. Once you have gone through the pain, you come out the other side you can then reeducate your machine and remodify it so that the next time you won't have to be triggered in the same way or on a lesser scale. In this way you can become empowered. It is truly in this empowerment that the authentic self can grow and become what God intended it to be. The authentic self is the presence of all the gifts God has given you along with the specialness and uniqueness of your real self. It is the jewel of your identity. It is the essence of your spirit. It is that which sets you aside from the others. It is your signature. Once you have achieved the awareness of your authentic self and you are comfortable with the surrendering of your pain you will then begin to see pain as a friend and teacher rather than an enemy whom you are continuing to run away from and hide. Once you have begun to modify and reeducate your machine you can begin to achieve what I have coined Personal Balance™. Personal Balance™ is the balance between the two selves, the machine and the real self. When the real self is in control it is in control of the machine and it is not being driven by the machine, it is not being protected by the machine. It is "being" and it uses the machine as a consultant when there is genuine danger to contend with. True balance is the state of grace. We must alter our perception of what is painful. We must learn to trust ourselves as we surrender into the black forest of pain. We must reevaluate our child-hood trauma and go into emotional spaces that we have spent a lifetime avoiding. We must reconnect with those earlier spaces of pain so as to go through them and in do-ing so, transcend the amount of energy that was necessary to hold the pain in. If you really think about it you'll discover that it takes a tremendous amount of emotional and psychic energy in order to harbor pain from one's self. Think about this. You are holding in the emotionally charged pain from yourself and you are coping and surviv-ing which takes more energy. All of this is unnecessary yet it is essentially what our machines do most of the time. We **_survive_** life, we don't **_live_** life.

THE INTERVIEW

("D" is Dr. French and "V" is Veronica)

D: Before you first knew about this model and this work that I've introduced to you, how did you think that you as a person were wired? In other words, how did you operate?

V: I don't think I thought of myself as being wired. I just was. I wouldn't have questioned my feelings or why I was feeling things or if there were things I was feeling that I wanted to change, but I don't think I thought of myself as being wired.

D: So then when you would smile or hide your feelings and on the inside you felt differently, maybe it's something you want to disguise, you wouldn't necessarily think of the inside one as being the real you and the outside one being the part of you that was hiding?

V: Not until after I'd heard your model.

D: But what would you have thought?

V: When I was being happy or if I was smiling or if I was listening to someone else, being a good friend, I was doing it for the other person, for my classmates, for whatever. It wasn't me dealing with my pain for myself, it was, oh there's Veronica, and you can always count on Veronica to be there for you, to be positive, to smile. But this created an uncomfortable situation because if something bad happened and I was upset, people didn't like that and they would say to me, "Veronica, what's wrong with you? You're never like this. If you're like this the rest of us are just going to fall apart." They got used to seeing me as someone positive or someone happy. And even to this day, even though I show my feelings and talk to people about negative things or situations or that fact that I'm not having a good day or I'm upset, people still don't necessarily like to hear it. "Oh Veronica, come on, you're the one we can always count on to get us through." So before it was kind of like alright I'll be there.

D: That's a big responsibility.

V: I thought it was the right thing to do.

D: Well, what's the right thing to do now?

V: The right thing to do is to be who you are. It's to express yourself, and in expressing yourself that's all of yourself. By doing that you're more than you were before and you can be there even more for the other person in being there for yourself

D: Talk to me about the model, the one I've introduced to you. Describe the model the way you understand it.

V: The way I understand it is that there's me, the real me, and there's a protective self that looks out for me and messes me up. There are core issues that we all have based on our own individual experiences, but the general model can be applied to anyone based on this is how I really feel and this is my protection looking out for me, but in my protection looking out for me it doesn't allow me to live fully in that moment or to express myself. It kind of hinders my expression of me and it plays down my ability to risk. It discourages that, based on paranoia, or something like that, in taking risks, it's a threat to this protection or if it doesn't like it. The big challenge it is to override that protection. To say yes, I know my machine is looking out for me, yes I understand and if it were necessary, I would rely on it, but in most cases it is not. I want to live for me and express this and experience this and I can't fully experience this if it is shielding me. I have to put my heart out there and I'm not going to die if I get hurt. It may be a painful process, but I'm not going to die, it's going to be something to grow from. Because the machine plays a game and it's really easy to listen to and believe. It plays a really good game so it's hard to say no. This is how I feel and you can talk and say all these things that could be true, that might be true, or maybe definitely are not true. But they sound good and are easy to buy into, but that is not what I want to do. I want to not buy into that garbage. I want to be how I am and feel how I feel and experience this.

D: Why did you allow it before? Why did you buy into the garbage before?

V: I thought it was the truth because it was coming from me.

D: Because you believed your machine.

V: Yeah, but I didn't know I was believing my machine although I thought that these were my thoughts in my head and I was helping myself.

D: So, that made the turn for you? How did you shift your thinking into understanding?

V: If you know something and you don't do anything about it you're kidding yourself or you're pretending. So after your model was presented to me and I was made aware of it to not recognize it or to not get involved with it was to live a lie or pretend.

D: What's the feeling like when you become aware of the fact through understanding the model that you have done this to yourself?

V: It's terrible. I resented myself because I realized that I had been treating myself very badly and I remember you gave me an image I think it was in high school and you were saying, "Veronica, you have to imagine that you are this little girl and you have just beaten her up and left her by the side of the road, but she is the truth and you have done this." I felt awful, really ugly that I had done that to myself. It's really terrible when you find out you haven't been taking care of yourself.

D: But you thought you were; and the machine thought it was.

V: Yeah.

D: So there's no malicious intention?

V: But it was malicious

D: How?

V: The outcome was malicious. I ended up being malicious to myself not knowing that but in not letting me be me, or feel this way, or do these things, and find out that I had left this precious child by the side of the road is not acceptable.

D: Where is the child now?

V: Center stage.

D: Where is the machine?

V: In the wings. It's still there, but the child is center and the machine is there and is very active and it still gets me, but it's not the same.

D: So you now know when it's talking?

V: I now know more. I can recognize it. It's still hard because I find that the more aware of it I get, the cleverer it becomes.

D: So as you learn more about yourself it learns also.

V: As I advance, so does it.

D: So you have to stay, basically, one step ahead of the machine?

V: So that means you're never done. It's never "I did it, the machine is gone. I went through one session and the machine has left and all I have to do is just be myself now." It's not easy like that. It's kind of ongoing and that presents more challenges. As you advance so does the machine. There's always something else to deal with or something else to work on or something else to be aware of.

D: Were you angry with your machine?

V: I was angry with myself, but I think that meant that I was angry at the machine.

D: For lying to you although it thought it was telling you the truth?

V: Because I think that I thought that I was the machine. That it wasn't like the machine is doing this and Veronica is doing this. It's Veronica who did this to herself.

D: That's what you thought?

V: Yes.

D: Now what would you say you think today?

V: What I think today is that I wouldn't have intentionally done that to myself. I didn't mean to leave myself by the side of the road and I wasn't aware of it and when I was aware of it, that's when changes came about that the machine was looking out for me and protecting me. So, I think that makes me look at it differently. That it wasn't Veronica doing this to Veronica it was Veronica's protection and the result of that protection was that state.

D: This is what I call surviving life rather than living.

V: Right, because I survived and it wasn't like I didn't have nice memories or good times, but it wasn't whole.

D: What percentage of the time, when you look back on it, do you think you were being the machine? Or what percentage of the time were you being authentic?

V: Probably 75% machine, but I think I felt that I came through the machine. That even if the machine was on you could still see me in my eyes maybe, or in something that I was doing. That a little bit of me could be seen.

D: That's very interesting. You've never said that before.

V: I never thought of that before. Yeah, that even the thought the machine was on was like, I'm here, and can you see me?

D: This was before, right?

V: Yeah, and whoever saw me I thought was very smart. Whoever recognized me got a lot of respect.

D: Then you were aware of the two selves before.

V: Maybe, just not in a conscious way. If someone could recognize Veronica, they were someone to be reckoned with.

D: A higher consciousness.

V: Yeah! Someone that I like and appreciated them for that; for being able to recognize me.

D: Recognize you even though you weren't center stage?

V: Yes. For being able to see me in the wings.

D: Why do you smile when you say that? Why did that delight you when somebody saw that?

V: Because someone saw me.

D: But when someone saw you and you were delighted, in other words, you wanted them to see you without you being center stage, why weren't you willing to come out center stage before so we could see you without having to look so hard?

V: I don't know. It must have been that it was too big of a risk.

D: But yet you were tickled and delighted when some of us could see you on the wings. And even that look on your face now, what is that look, what's the feeling? You're doing it again. You have that warm smile, what does that smile mean?

V: I'm thinking of incidents that happened and it was usually always older people who would do this. It was kind of like they would see me and they would give me the look I'm giving you.

D: But tell me, what's the feeling? What does it make you feel like when you've been discovered?

V: It's special.

D: Now that's different than when they found out because you're not threatened.

V: No, not at all.

D: Obviously, but some people are because they have thought that they have kept it pretty well hidden. So, in a way is that like a test? If we could see you're special, does that mean you could now risk more?

V: Probably.

D: Does that make us safe because we saw you and we appreciate you?

V: Yes, it's the appreciation.

D: So when we see you we are honoring that you're special and in doing that does that disarm your machine?

V: In some way.

D: To me, the way to work it is to treat people to look for where the person is in the wings and not respond to the machine. That's the work because if you respond to just a person's machine you could have justification but wanting not to get too close to them, but if you look into the wings beyond where the machine is and not take their machine personally, I think you could treat people better than they deserve and you will find their specialness. When you find their specialness, you will disarm their machine, and they'll feel more comfortable coming center stage.

V: But it's a lot easier for people to say, "Look at this, look at this attitude. Screw this person." It's a lot easier to write a person off than to take the time to sit down and look at yourself to look inside them.

D: I think it's very hard to find the special Veronica when Veronica's machine is glaring, is being bitchy, abrasive, rude, insensitive, unfair, unjust, manipulative, deceitful. It's very hard in the presence of that machine going off, to look for the softness and the specialness because it feels dangerous when that thing is going off. So, when I'm trying to look for you my machine is telling me to back off, watch it French, she is getting ugly, you better let me protect you, and I have to actually stop myself from defending myself and say to myself, Veronica doesn't mean this. She's in the wings. It's like the Wizard of Oz at the end of the movie when the dog, Toto, finds the real wizard. The machine wizard is on the screen bellowing our all those orders and everyone is terrified and the real wizard is behind the curtains and you know what the machine says, "Pay no attention to that man behind the curtain." That's what I'm trying to work on in my life is treating people better than they deserve. It's hard sometimes. I can tell you I want to do it, I can tell you I intend to do it, but I'll tell you there are times when I meet certain peoples machines that for a moment I'm triggered and I just can't look for that specialness because it seems to dangerous again. It just does and I think when it looks like it's definitely meant for me, like if I say something and someone responds and they glare at me, that really feels like more of a dangerous attack – I believe my machine's lie!

V: But there are times when you'll engage with certain personalities like that when you want to respond in the same manner. You'd like to go off on them. You'd like to be able to get angry and "stand up for myself." I'm going to stand up for myself. And that's another thing that a lot of times I think people talk about standing up for themselves, but the place in which they do it from is drive, its machine driven. It doesn't come from a place that says I love myself. I care about myself and I want to connect with you in that way or I don't want to have this kind of conversation with you. I think that is hard to because, especially for me, because if someone is very aggressive and very knowledgeable or comes off in that way and they're speaking to me in a certain tone it's as easy to buy into another person's machine as it is to buy into your own. Because your machine talks a good game so that's why you believe it and listen to it and that's why is operates so much of the time. And if it's that easy to buy into your own machine, it's extremely easy to buy into someone else's.

D: I agree. Can you name some times that you've caught yourself that you were triggered and you were able to catch yourself; can you name any successes you've had?

V: The most basic thing I can think of, is if I'm thinking in my head about a chain of events, about something that happened, or about something that might happen, and I hear my head creating a situation to buy into that hasn't happened yet, that isn't real, that, of course could happen, it is possible, but it has not, it may not, I can say this isn't real.

D: That's the machine going off. What it's doing is it's trying to protect you.

V: Like prepare me. It's trying to prepare me for all these different scenarios.

D: And it does it with such passion.

V: It doesn't say, "Veronica, you can handle whatever scenario comes along if you're you." Because that's the truth. It doesn't say that.

D: Fundamentally, the machine does not believe that you are okay just the way you are.

V: Because if it believed that, it wouldn't be around.

D: What would you say the machine, fundamentally believes?

V: I think the machine, fundamentally believes that I'm special and that I need to be guarded.

D: So, it does see you as special?

V: I think it does.

D: That's good. But why doesn't it believe that your specialness is enough to be wonderful, to be received?

V: Because it's like that vulnerability and that innocence if you give that to the world, they'll tear you apart.

D: Because it has evidence that is the case.

V: Right. You can just put yourself out there like that. It's a jungle, they're animals. They, whoever they are, other specials out in the world are going to tear you apart. I guess it's because I knew, look at me, I'm right here, through the machine. I knew was in there and I knew that it knew it too. From me being on the wings, it knew I was there and it was doing the dance for me. It's like I was the understudy from my own experience.

D: You knew what you wanted to say so the machine would prepare you, this is how your particular machine works, and it would prepare you for all the different scenarios that could happen.

V: That's the most basic example of how I stop it. Because my machine starts throwing out scenarios in my head and I know it's not coming out from a real place. It's jumping ahead.

D: So, how do you stop it?

V: This isn't real and I tell myself, "What is real? I am here. This is how I feel right now. Whatever may happen may happen."

D: And I am going to trust myself that when it gets there I'll be okay. Now when you say that does the machine still try to say, "Now, no, no, it won't be okay?" When you go to center stage does the machine automatically go off stage?

V: I think it depends on the situation how easily it leaves, how much it fights, how much it tries to push me out of the spotlight. We may argue a little bit, especially in issues of confrontation. Especially. It would fight with me over the spotlight. I've gotten better at this, but I remember in high school too, if issues of confrontation came up there's dialogue that goes on in my head, "Are you going to do this? I don't know if you should do this. Veronica!" It's back and forth, and then, finally, it's I'm going. Just open the door and dive in. I'm not going to think about it, don't think just do.

D: So, one metaphor I've used is I see the machine as a loving yet somewhat paranoid parent and the special Veronica is the fragile vulnerable child. Now, a child must separate from its' parent. Most people don't do that because they believe the machine to be them and they believe that since the machine is center stage that must be who they are and what's in the wings must just be afterthoughts or residue of what they really are. So, when you become aware and really recognize, what I call, ***the perpetual lie*** that you've lied to yourself because the machine and you make a pact, I believe at the moment of the original pain when you got hurt that the machine basically says "That really hurt, didn't it, when mom didn't give us that or when dad glared at us?" That's our mom and dad that really hurt. I'll help you any time anybody does this to you for the rest of your life and I will make sure to protect you.

V: It's a good deal.

D: It's a good deal. So you go play Veronica, and I'll watch for you. I call that the lie, because the lie to me is, once you make the pact with yourself to do that, it's like signing with the devil in a way because you are selling out your soul. You're giving your specialness away to the machine because this definitely hurt when daddy glared at you so let's protect you now. Then, you make the pact and I believe you, and then forget that you made the pact which is what I call the beginning of the perpetual lie. Can you remember the moment of your original pain? Do you know when that was? Is there a moment for you or is there a context that you find this in? Or, maybe even yet, how do you know what your issue is? What is your core issue?

V: My core issue has a lot to do with approval from others. It has to do with my father and not feeling important to my father but the way I frame it is in my childhood. When I look at my childhood, I feel I had a very good childhood, a very happy childhood. I had moments of pain in grammar school. Mostly with my peers, my peers and my father; bullies at school or arguments or fights, just cruelty between kids.

D: Everything that the machine tells you is a lie with the exception of genuine danger, where someone's going to physically hurt you, is aiming their car at you, is going to shoot a gun at you, a knife, etc. Literally, anything else is a lie. That still is amazing to me to say out loud.

V: Because it is very hard to believe.

D: That's right. It's very hard to believe. And, for some people, it's impossible to believe because they've lived their life center stage with the machine being there and I believe it's a codependent relationship. Like a child has with a parent. The mother won't let the child leave home and she's protecting her until she's in her forties and she's doing it under the guise of loving her deeply, but the child is forty-three years old, never dated, never married, doesn't have a life, but yet is surviving it and that's a sick relationship. That child who is now a grown woman does not have a life. That child needs to separate from that mother, but that mother will never let that child open that door and go out into the world because she's convinced her that it's dangerous. And she continues to bring home evidence, the mother, that is, that there is danger out there. By showing her headlines in the newspaper, letting her see that there are car accidents, fires, tragedies, riots, and gun battles. So, that child will never go outside. I believe that's how people live their lives. They never get to go outside. And when you go outside what you get to do is risk. Now, today you're not afraid of risking, you're not afraid of showing up in your special-ness. Obviously, you understand that you're center stage. Other times it's still scary for you so how do you deal with that? What are those times? Give me a time that's safe, that you can now go center stage that you wouldn't have done before and give me a time that's still scary for you center stage.

V: I confront people more; I express my pain a hell of a lot more.

D: But, what if we say "Oh, Veronica, I don't like to see you that way. Where's the happy girl? Why don't you smile?"

V: That's hard to hear, but it's just like, shut up.

D: You're disappointing your fans.

V: Exactly! That's how I feel sometimes. I'm disappointing my fans. And that's terrible because they love me and I love them back. That's hard to hear, but I listen to it and I just say, "No, I have to do this and if you can't see me do it, that's fine, you can leave and if you want to come sit here on the couch with me in the dark, you can do that too." And I catch myself apologizing to them.

D: So that's easier for you.

V: It's easier for me to show my pain, easier for me to confront people.

D: What would be hard for you then?

V: Hard for me is still believing that someone who approaches you is extremely driven and their drivenness throws me.

D: Their drivenness with such an intensity side swipes you, knocks you off, and derails you. And then, the shock of the intensity of their being driven then puts you in a place where you are absolutely fumbling inside to manage yourself. That really upsets your machine.

V: It's very hard for me to believe they're not doing that and you don't take this personally. Inside their specialness is tied up and gagged in a back closet. Have compassion, look for them, and go over there, it's extremely hard. And what else is extremely hard is for me to not believe in what they're saying; for me to not buy into what they are saying. It's extremely hard for me not to allow that segment of doubt to come over me.

D: How does the sideswiping relate to your issue? How does it relate to your childhood? How did you get sideswiped there?

V: That's a good question. I can't remember.

D: I think it might have been as simple as you having this extraordinary sensitivity as a child and daddy may have walked into the room being very intense because he's a powerful and very bright man, he's very intense. He may have just said something to you with a command and authoritative voice, a very powerful voice that would have just sideswiped you at that moment. And it would have made you uncomfortable and frightened and rather than show that to him you would have hidden it. Why?

V: If I'm out there, if I'm center stage, it catches me off guard if other people aren't. Because it is so natural for me to be center stage now, that it's hard for me to realize that not everyone else is operating center stage. Because it's so natural for me to be center stage now that it's hard for me to realize, "No, Veronica, all these other people are operating on their machines. Don't take their words as coming from a place of authenticity." It's easy to think we're all in this together. I'm out here, we're all out here.

D: When you talked about people seeing your specialness, particularly old people, and it delighted you to be discovered, the question I want to ask is when you were in the wings before, were you able to see other people's specialness?

V: That's a really good question. I was able to see other people's pain. I don't know if I was able to see other people's specialness.

D: But seeing their pain was seeing their realness because that was their feeling. Seeing someone's pain is seeing the real self. But you were not able to see the person in a state of specialness because it took the pain that they were feeling inside to draw you to it.

V: And before, if I had seen someone in pain, I would have gone over and talked to them and been with them, but I don't think I felt it with them. Now, I feel it with them.

D: What I know to be true is that when I'm center stage, I believe that other people, even though they don't know about the model of other people's machines, are going to be disarmed significantly by me showing up center stage. So, when you say it's still hard for you to believe that other people's machines are going off, those machines aren't going off as much as they would because clearly they don't perceive danger.

V: But, wouldn't it, in a sense, be a threat to certain machines to have me be real?

D: Yes. Well how about using my metaphor of the mother that's protecting her forty-three year old daughter by keeping her hidden inside. It would be like a healthy woman coming to the door saying, "My name is Jane Smith and I understand you have a daughter about my age. I'm married, here are my three children. I have a wonderful job and career. I'm very spiritually grounded and I've been living on the outside for many years. That's a reminder to the mother and the daughter of what could have been.

V: So, that is a threat. It's a trigger.

D: That's a trigger for some machines. Yes. Because it's a reminder of exposure. In fact, when some people show feelings that's a trigger for some machines. I believe this, when you show up center stage you're making a demand on anybody you talk to, in a sense. Not a demand like you're pushing them, but it is a demand in the sense you are inviting them to be center stage. And that's a perceived threat by the machine. But I believe if you stay there long enough in a loving authentic place, that machine can find nothing wrong. It's like at the airport when they have those portable metal detectors, the machine basically goes through you with a fine tooth comb and if it finds no weapons, or any evidence of danger, then it really can't stay activated because it's based upon what it perceives to be dangerous.

V: And it's so ironic because it all comes back to you, this whole model, everything that happens, all the interactions that happen, it all comes back to you.

No matter who hurt you in your childhood, no matter what your core issues were, or who did what to you, it all comes back to you. It all is with you. And, "Oh, this person wasn't real with me." Well maybe that was because you weren't being real with yourself. I mean it all comes back to you. It's a lot.

D: Yes it does. In fact, I distinctly remember many times saying that I thought people were phony, I did not like their insincerity, I didn't like people being bullies, or people who were manipulative and the truth is, I'm every one of those things, and I've been every one of those things. I want to say "It ain't pretty, but it's the truth." So everything I've accused you of or thought of you, I am myself. And I also know this to be true, that the way I treat you and the rest of the people is the way I want to be treated. So, I'm real attentive, I like being real sensitive and compassionate. There are times I'm that way and it's my machine. Like you said, as you've learned, your machine learns how to disguise itself through sounding authentic, through doing nice things, that I've discovered I have motivations behind that later on through feedback, etc., being aware that was conditional. I was doing it for approval. I was doing it to be liked. It wasn't done freely. I think it's just an amazing thing, it does come back, but the part I know to be true now is that I'm secretly treating people the way I want to be treated. And the other part I know to be true is that I am every one of those bullies that bullied me. I'm every one of those manipulators who manipulated me. And I've got every bit of a mask as I thought other jerks in the world had. I'm the jerk. I've been the jerk. And when I'm in a loving, authentic place, I really believe my ability to see you in the side lines is a really real easy to do. But when I'm being a jerk, I believe all I can see is your machine, and when I don't honor my specialness, I can't honor yours. And probably the most frightening people in the world are the sociopaths or the ones that are so pathological that they have no remorse, no authentic and they have no conscience. And when you don't have a conscience, I don't believe you have someone in the wings, I believe they've left the stage all together. Those are the most dangerous people in the world because they are 100% machine. Saddam Hussein was a 100% killing machine. I believe he's like a shark that's swimming in the water and whatever goes into his mouth he'll eat. There's no discrimination. There's no sensitivity to the fact that what he just ate was a child and what he just ate was fragile or handicapped or disabled. I believe there's no discrimination. That's a frightening person to me. Somebody who doesn't have a self is frightening. You see if yourself is in the sidelines you don't seem as dangerous to me as when you tell me you're the machine and then I know that self is gone. The absence of self is a 100% presence of the machine. That is, to me, the beginning of evil. Good to me is the presence of self. Even if it's disguised or hidden in the room by the sick mother, it's still there. That's why, I believe that there's hope for us because I believe that most people are waiting to be liberated. They're waiting to be reborn, but the machines run them. My machine has run me in the past, and to some degree it still does, but I feel I have much more empowerment today over it because when things happen to me I can tell what's going on with me and how it's related to my original pain – that knowledge is power.

V: And it's a lot of work.

D: It's a lot of work, you're right. And some people don't want to do all the work. Why do you want do to the work? And describe that. How does that work for you? Why do you want to do it?

V: Because I want me. I want to do it because I want me and I want to experience my life as me the fullest way I can to be a whole person, to be that connected, to be that grounded. Because when you are in that place, it's beautiful, but I think it is still a lot of work. Like I said, it all comes back to you. So, if you look at things that happened in your life you have to go back to your child-hood and the pain. You can't get away from the pain, you have to go through it. You have to recognize it. And I like the way you say if you try, that's what's important. It's not successes and failures. To ignore it when you know it ex-ists, that's more of a failure that if you're trying. It's not smooth sailing, but the effort is there. The intention is there. The will is there. And I think that is what's good. The work is really important because you're giving yourself your life. You're allowing yourself to live.

D: You're giving yourself your life. That's a beautiful phrase. You're giving your-self your life. What was the machine giving you them? It was giving you a way of surviving your life.

V: Yes.

D: Where do you think the machine came from? I believe it's wired into the organism.

V: The machine came from me.

D: Right. But I believe everybody's machine has been passed on through the generations and its part of what is built into the organism to help it survive.

V: It finds its' place. It finds a reason to exist, but yeah, it came from me. I don't know the moment when it was but I see myself sitting in a sand box and hearing this little voice because it sounds rational, it sounds so logical and it's like of course, okay, that sounds good. And then it seems like once the machine gets the okay, it just takes off. It's not conservative in the area that it protects. It kind of just takes over and runs the house. It doesn't stay handy or hired on reserve, it takes over.

D: That's true. And it sounds good because it sounds like you. And it makes sense and yet we don't question its' interpretation of reality.

V: The thing is we don't question the machine we question ourselves.

D: That's good. What's that about? We don't question the machine we question ourselves. But isn't it like if your parents told us something when we were little, don't we think, well, something must be wrong with me because mom and dad think it's this way. So, therefore if I disagree with it something must be wrong because they must know. They're bigger; they're my mom and dad, they're protecting me, they're in charge. So, we just give it away?

V: Because I think that it's the same thing as if you're driving somewhere and the machine says, "Where are you going?" And it's at you and you just say, "I'm going to be alright because I believe in God and I've got me and it's going to be alright. If I get hurt, I will go through pain, I will feel it, and I will grow. I'm going to be happy, I'm going to be please, and I'm going to laugh. Machine what can you present to me?" But the machine can talk it up, "You know, I heard there was an accident on the 405" there is all kinds of stuff going on. It can just talk at you, and you say you know that you're right because if the machine says, "What are you going to do?" or "Where are you going?" and you just have a simple answer it's like "Why do you like chocolate?" I don't know, it doesn't matter why, I just do. It's me. So, it sounds so simple compared to this essay that the machine has written, and you're thinking, wait a minute, you do sound better, you do sound like you know more. All I know is that I like chocolate, I don't really know why I like chocolate and it can just talk you into a circle.

D: I asked my daughter Courtney, "What do you like?" and she said "I like chocolate" and I said "Why?" and she even laughed like I was being silly and she said, "Because I do." And to her it was like I don't have to explain this. I don't even have to describe it because any justification or any description or explanation would be the machine. Children aren't doing that. But there's a point where it starts to shift that they start doing it. And I think as parents you have an opportunity. I think we have an opportunity to validate their feelings and to honor their specialness, so in that context I believe that all the parents were doing the best they could and it was their machines that were raising their children and that one must forgive their parents because they were not maliciously trying to hurt them, they were just doing what they thought was right and they were giving their child the same machine that was running their lives. So really your parent is only giving you the same information it gives itself.

V: And that's why you pass on a dysfunction.

D: You pass on the machine language.

V: Because it's what you know.

D: It's what you know to be true, and if your parents are living it, it must be the way to live. I love that statement you made that's a really wonderful statement, "We believe the machine, but we don't believe ourselves." And today, what would you say. I don't want to say it for you. How would you say that same statement today?

V: I would say, I believe myself, but it's not easy. That's what I would say. And I don't always win. I, to this day, can still get talked into a good game

D: Knowing what you know and knowing that you're on to that damn machine.

V: It can still get me. And that's when it gets frustrating.

D: That's why I believe you have to stay one step ahead of it. How would you call it? That's my way of phrasing it. What would your language be? What's the work that you need to do to continue growing and honoring yourself and not to be bamboozled by that machine?

V: Have a stronger belief in myself. As strong and as hard as it can go off, I believe that strongly in myself. I'm that strongly grounded. My belief in myself is stronger than my belief in the machine.

D: Right. But what's the work that you have to do with the machine? What is your work with the machine?

V: Well, it's still recognizing it when it's working. Because there are plenty of times that I know that I don't recognize it. I mean, I recognize it more than I ever did before, but there are still times that I'm sure it just slides by me. It's recognizing when it is working and then taking the time to ask why is this happening and what is this about. And to override the machine's request that I not feel unknown feelings, uncomfortable feelings. That's as well as saying, "No we don't know what this is or where it came from, but it's there let's get it out." It doesn't like that. So, I think I don't like that. The machine doesn't like it when I feel those feelings so I think I don't like it when I feel those feelings.

D: What threatens the machine doesn't necessarily threaten you.

V: But I can think it does.

D: But you think it does because the machine who you've been indebted to and who's protected you all these years and you think it's you, you believe it. Did you have any sense of having wasted time or was there any sense of a loss when you finally are aware that you've been in the wings, you haven't been you, you finally go center stage, and do you have a feeling of any mourning or any loss or any grieving?

V: I grieved over the little girl on the side of the road who was beaten up. I didn't feel any loss of resentment of time because I was fifteen or something when I first realized it. I know I can say I'm being real, I'm in a real time, but I feel like how far I've come, there's plenty more. I could be that much more real. There's more.

D: How has this model and perspective on yourself, helped you to see other people? Hasn't it given you a sense of power or insight into other people because you now can see when they're being the machine and when they're being real? Can't you see more of them or more about them?

V: I see how much less of them I'm really seeing. Because I'm aware of how much the machine is on.

D: So, what would you say if I asked you what do you want? What do you still want right now?

V: I want what I have and I want more of it. I feel like I want to be where I am, but I want to continue on this road, continue on this path, and continue on this journey. In saying that, I'm asking for more. More pain and more struggles.

D: Tell me about pain and tell me about what's your willingness to feel pain or feel those kinds of feelings today.

V: My willingness is much greater. Now that I look at the first time we did a session years ago when you tried to get me to go deeper inside of myself what I called central supply.

D: The central supply you're referring to is a metaphor of you going down inside your feelings, where all the boxes of feelings are stored up.

V: Right. I didn't know how to get there. You had to try to get me to get there, but I didn't think I knew how. Now I know how. I'm much more willing. It doesn't make it any easier to sit down and say "Alright, here we go." But, the fact that I'm able, the capability is there; I can do it for myself. But I don't know how if I'm afraid of all the times I need to do that.

D: Were you afraid of feeling pain before?

V: Yes, I put the elephant in the closet that you say, we put this big elephant in the closet and then you go through it, and it ends up being a mouse. Why? Because it was dark, or it was bad, or scary, or it was very unknown

D: Because you have such a need to know and to understand which is really driven by your machine. That was a real trigger for you if you didn't know what it was. So essentially, if the machine can't tell what it is that you're going to feel, in other words you have a feeling and you say to the machine in the sidelines, "I need to feel this. I what to feel this," and the machine says, "What is it?" and you say, "It's pain." If the machine can't label it and know the boundaries of it, and exactly what it is, it won't let you embrace it. It's got to be in control of it.

V: Okay, I'm sad because my cat got hit by a car.

D: Right. The machine would let you feel that. Or if you stepped on a tack and said this hurt.

V: If somebody dies, cry all you want. Loss, it hurts. Some unknown funky, "What is this?" I don't know. Where did it come from? "I don't know. Get rid of it."

D: A lot of people, I think, live with the illusion that if they store it inside and forget about it, it goes away. I've seen hundreds of people do that, and end up in a place where their garage is full. Their central supply, their garage, is full of boxes and they are out of room. And when you're out of room, physically, emotionally; you're in trouble. Because then what happens is like what one lady told me she was shopping at Vons and she looked at the cantaloupe and she started to cry. Well, the cantaloupe has absolutely nothing to do with making her cry, but she's so full that it just came upon its' own because It's trying to slip out. The body finally says, "I think when you're loaded up like that, machine or no machine, it's coming out, get out of the way." And that's when people are frightened because that's when their machine can't even compose them or it can't even contain them. That's when people feel like they are on the edge of a nervous breakdown. And in a sense, they are on the edge of a breakdown. Their machine's ability to contain them has broken down. What's really emerging is all the pent up pain that they've had for years. That's really sad. Then I've actually met some people who metaphorically are building, I hear them hammering away. They're trying to make another storage area. I say, "What are you doing?" and they say, "I'm building another garage." And I say, "You can't. God gave you one space inside to hold things in and that's all there is." But they go on building thinking they're going to be able to have more room to store. Pretty frightening. And some people live that way. They live with a central supply that's loaded and they live way up in their head, pure machine, while I call the remains of them are no longer in the wings as you call it. The remains of them are underneath all the boxes in central supply.

V: And there's no room. They can't feel anything. They're stuffed in there. They can't feel like if it's like that.

D: That's right, but they can survive it. To me, that's living death. I don't think that's life. Surviving life is like being dead.

V: And that's so hard to survive like that. You're living and their trying to maintain and there's so much pain in them they don't know what to do.

D: What essentially happens, clinically, is that when you have that many boxes on top of you, you are functionally depressed. And the depression is like somebody put a big blanket over the central supply, which numbs the whole thing. So, when they think of themselves, they don't feel anything. Feeling nothing is depression. In order for that person to get well, they have to remove the blanket of depression, they have to open the boxes of anger and then they have to release the pain. And actually, at the end of the pain, the end of the rainbow is the treasure of where the real self is.

V: But it feels kind of good. It's that cleansing. Even though it's hard and scary, when you're in it, it kind of feels good.

D: The trick is getting in it, because even bringing you down into central supply your machine was trying to rationalize it, think about it, What is this? Why are we going here? What am I supposed to feel? Sorry I can't do it, this isn't working. I have this other belief that everybody is aware whether it's conscious or unconscious about what I'm doing or what I'm saying. In other words, I believe that when I interact with somebody they can feel whether I'm being sincere or not. Even if they are largely the machine, I believe that the impression I leave or the impact I make is recorded either consciously or unconsciously.

V: We can sense or we have an awareness of those actions.

D: Yes. I knew there were times when someone was being the machine even years ago, but I didn't know the model the way I know it today. I could tell I could feel something funny. I've seen children back off from adults because they don't feel comfortable. I've seen dogs and cats back off from certain people that they're not comfortable with. So, I believe people can tell whether it's conscious or unconscious that they're receiving, and I think a lot of times it's unconscious. In other words, I might walk away from them, they may not exactly know what happened, but they have a feeling that's unconscious about me

V: If they could put it into words, it's like something isn't right.

D: Correct. But I think if they're around me long enough and I'm the machine enough, I think they begin to make a decision that might become conscious that I'm not somebody to be safe with. Because I remember years ago a very close friend telling me that they felt there were times I was insincere. And I remember them even telling me at a moment when I felt I was being sincere. But looking back on it, now that I know what I know, even the time I was starting to cry with them was not sincere. What I discovered about myself is because I had so many of those bullies in my life, I learned how to show pain to them, to be a victim.

V: Like, have mercy?

D: Correct. And I believe that my machine began to use this pain or my expression of the pain as a way of coping. So, that if somebody did something to me that the machine perceived as being a bully or dangerous my machine might try to disarm it by showing that I was hurt, and I might even cry. And what I discovered is that is how I would buy that was real. I mean my God, Veronica, I'm crying. How could that be the machine? And I want to tell you a quick story about a patient of mine who had about fifty different affairs, while he was married, with prostitutes. When his wife found out she was taking her baby and she was going to leave. He was in the office with me and her and he began to sob, not cry, sob He was dripping from his nose because he was crying and sobbing so hard. Well, it didn't feel right to me, so I said to his wife; "Do you feel like you're being sold?" and she said "Yes." And he looked at me like he hated me because I exposed him. My point is that's how clever the machine is and now when my friend said that to me it really angered me at the time. I thought, "How dare you, this is me. How dare you."

V: But it's the machine that's trying to convince them.

D: But it was also more evidence for my machine to say "Look, French, you just put your guts out there." It leads me to believe I went center stage and I didn't

V: It lead you to believe that you went center stage and look what you got back, so don't try and go center stage again.

D: There's a lot of evidence to say it doesn't work. And you know what I know today and I wish I could tell that person, because I don't even know where they are, "You were right. I was being phony and I was being manipulative under the guise of sincerity and I'm sorry, but I obviously was threatened and that's one posture that I take if I'm injured if I believe in injuries there. I look like I'm hurt and what it usually has done for me is stop the bullet from hitting me. The truth is, I'm not being real, but it looks real." One of those things again I've got to say, "It ain't pretty, but it's true." And you know that somehow saying it frees me up.

V: It feels good.

D: It does. It does.

V: Because you're being honest with yourself and you're being honest with other people.

D: And now one of the little things I do for myself as a way of helping me is I pretend when I meet somebody new I tell myself, "They know all of this about me. They know I could manipulate them, extort their feelings, connive them, deceive them, and bully them. They know I could do that to them in talking to me so they're on to me."

V: So, your real self tells you that, right.

D: Yes.

V: How could you tell the difference between your real voice talking and your machine talking?

D: The difference to me is the subjective feeling that I have inside my body when I'm saying it. I know I've done what I call this anchoring, of this emotional photograph. When I'm being me and I get evidence from you and other people that I'm in a wonderful place, that they're seeing my specialness, I'm center stage, I'm being authentically me. I've tried to photograph that, subjectively, so I know what the picture is. That becomes home base. So, I have a subjective feeling and I have a knowingness about what the space is. So, anything other than that is a subtle version of my machine coping. Because you know what, when I'm really being me, I'm no longer an issue, I'm no longer wondering if I'm alright, I just am. There are times I absolutely am doing what I am supposed to do for someone and it's real and it's received by them and I feel like it's what I'm supposed to do. I'm not even thinking about, "Gee, is this okay or not," it is just okay and I know it. There's a knowingness that comes with it. It really gets back to what you were saying earlier about trusting yourself. I think that's what's so sad is for years I didn't trust myself.

V: It's hard.

D: It is hard. You know why? Because of what I told you it's like, what I call, the best kept secret and that is you only have one self, every time it gets hurt, it gets smaller and it was the size of a dinner plate and now it's the size of a dime and one day the machine says "You better not only stay on the sidelines, you better go back stage and wait in one of the dressing rooms because if anybody shatters that dime we're dead, and that's it. No one is going to hurt you, I love you and I've been protecting you for many years, now you take that dime and you go in there." You know it's like your parent telling you, "Honey, I love you, you'd better do this." You don't challenge that until one day I said, "You know what, I can't go in the room," and the machine said, "What do you mean you can't go in the room?" I said, "I'll suffocate in there, I can't, I won't. I don't care. I just don't care, I'm coming out." And when I went out, I discovered nobody killed me.

V: Because you're not a plate. What we're made of, what our feelings are, this resilient fiber and people think we're going to break. How can you break?

D: Because people think that there's only so much of themselves because each time they've gotten hurt, the pain is diminishing them, it's making them smaller.

V: Instead of being more of them.

D: Well, because the more pain they have, the more women who've broken their hearts, or the more men who have done this or that, the more they say, "I can't risk this again." You know why? Because each time it happens they don't think they can make it the next time. It's almost like as you get older you can't make the trip. It's like, "I don't know if I can do this again. I don't know if I can walk the hundred flights of stairs again." So, you just sit down. And the truth is, there is a ***never ending supply of us.*** There is a resiliency that's there forever. In fact, I think when you risk again; you become even more empowered because what you're doing is educating your machine, and telling it that it didn't happen. And that's what the machine needs. It needs to be reprogrammed, reeducated. That happens by risking by the real self.

V: Do we view our machine as our enemy?

D: Yes. And I've had some people in therapy tell me "French, let's kill the damn thing. When are we going to get rid of it?"

V: But we can't kill it.

D: No. We don't want to kill it. We need it.

V: Just not very often?

D: I would say we need it, truthfully, probably if you're on the freeway and somebody goes to cut you off and you've got to protect yourself.

V: It's like reflex instinct, you need it in you.

D: But that's the way it's supposed to be. It's supposed to go on like getting a puff of air in your eye when you blink your eye. The machine works as the blinking response.

V: But isn't that all instinct?

D: Yes. It's wired in. See, I believe it is even passed on between parents to child. I don't know how to prove that, but maybe it's in the DNA, but mommy and daddy's machines that are encoded in their nervous systems get passed on to little Veronica and she takes that plus what she observes in her environment as a child and the combination of that, the genetic part, the environmental part, and what she experiences herself in the world all cause her machine to develop into what it will become. I really believe that. It's passed on. I've seen my second child, Ashley, who's a lot like me. Her machine acts like my machine. I used to think that twenty percent was genetic and you could probably mold the other eighty. Now I believe 80% is genetic and you might mold the other 20%.

V: You're kidding.

D: No. They come out that way. They are that way. The pregnancies are different. Cindy would tell me they felt different inside. When they come out and that little person that they are when they're a baby and all of a sudden you see them emerge and you start to see their personality, that's it. Then you can guide it. You can offer it interpretation, you obviously love it, and guide it, but it's set that way and I had no idea until I had children, until I could see the difference. Same parents, different pregnancy, different baby. Why does one react one way, and why does the other act this way? What's that about? I think it's absolutely amazing to think that the moment of conception could have been one minute earlier, four hours later and a totally different baby. The possibilities are unlimited. But I think it's a great responsibility we have as parents. I believe my responsibility to my children is for me to work on myself and to also introduce them to it. I have found out my kids have been afraid of my machine and didn't like it when it yelled or when it was angry. It's like a child comes into a room, and the mother and father are thinking of divorcing and the mother is crying and the little four year old says, "Mommy, are you alright?" And she quickly wipes the tears, smiles, and says, "No honey, I'm fine. I just had something in my eye." That child knows that is not true.

V: But it's getting conflicting messages.

D: Yes it is. And the message is: What my authentic is feeling is that mommy was sad, but mommy (mommy's machine) is saying no, I'm fine.

V: So, I must be wrong.

D: I must be wrong, it's my mommy.

V: So, we doubt ourselves?

D: We doubt ourselves because mommy wasn't being honest with herself. Can you blame mommy? No. Why? Because mommy's intention was to not hurt you. She thought it would hurt you if she told you the truth. So, her protecting you actually caused you to doubt yourself. She's protecting you out of a wonderfully good intention because it never occurs to her that telling you the truth is good for you. "Yes, honey, mommy is sad and she's hurt right now, but she'll be fine, she just needs to cry. Would you like to sit here with me and let me hold you?"

V: It's what it is.

D: Exactly. When you just said that it made me think to myself "Isn't it sad that here this mother is just trying to protect her baby from feeling pain because she doesn't want to hurt her baby, but by protecting her baby she's lying to her baby. Her baby sees the lie, her baby doubts herself and the baby believes the lie. Now, if your mother or father, which is the closest thing to God, tells you that's the reality, then that's the reality. So, twenty five years later, I bring the mother and daughter together and the mother says "Yes, I remember that moment, honey, it was just because I was divorcing your dad and I didn't want to hurt you," and she cries and says, "But mommy, I knew that you were sad, why did you lie to me?"

V: Isn't she angry?

D: A little bit, but when she finds out what the intention was, it was out of love, and then they forgive each other. But see, it would take an opportunity to bring them together to talk about it. They wouldn't just bring it up unless they were so motivated to do so. That's why with sexual abuse, many children feel responsible because, if your daddy does something to you, it must be something about you, or because of you.

V: Because they're doing it to you. Sounds personal.

D: And it's your father. So, it must be you. And then, of course, some people even feel guilty because they experienced a form of closeness and that's really ambiguous. So, parents have an incredible responsibility, but you see fundamentally we all have a responsibility. I believe it's to be responsible for ourselves, and we're not. That's why my favorite expression, even though I don't like saying it, but it's true, is that machines are running the world. The machines are getting into power. The machines are making decisions. It's not based on what's authentic; it's based on what's driven. It's based on coping; on surviving. But it's not about what's real. So, where do you find real?

V: Me, I find real, you mean outside of myself?

D: Yes.

V: I find real at the ocean, in the sky, and in children.

D: Animals?

V: Yes.

D: It's funny; you didn't bring up any adults.

V: I mean I do, but if there is that place where you have to go get in touch with it, I wouldn't go to a cocktail party. That's not where I would go to find real. I'd go to find real at the ocean of I'd go take Christian who's six out to the park and talk to her. I wouldn't go to the cocktail party. I mean I'd go if I wanted to; it would be fun, but if I felt the need to be reconnected with something like that.

D: How does going to the ocean feed you in the wings?

V: I feel it's good for the soul. I'd go there. It's the constancy, the rhythm. It's God, it's big, it's spiritual, it's here, and it's the noise and the motion. It's the consistency that no matter what's going on, it's alright.

D: In a sense, you're making your statement also about the real self no matter what the machine is doing. It's okay because it's real, but there's a point where it starts to suffocate. I guess that' the point where some people either fight for themselves or they don't. Because I know when I was on my way to the dressing room I thought that there was something wrong with it. In a way, it's challenging your own parent.

V: I'm sure there are people who don't think that they can challenge it. Who doesn't know that they have that choice to challenge the machine? I don't know if everyone realizes that they have that opportunity; they have that choice.

D: No, I don't think so.

V: When you're talking about the specialness, that's the one thing about the kids in South Africa that I felt, with their eyes. They would be sitting, and I would look at them and if I smiled, they would sit up. It was like somebody saw me, somebody recognized me, somebody paid attention to me. And I guess that's because it was special to me when I was younger, if someone could see that in me, if I see it is them, they feel that and that's the one thing that I was just so struck by. Whether it's at school counseling somebody on the floor, or that we just all hurt. We all hurt so much as a human family, we have that shared common experience, and I feel like we're connected in so many ways, but that's definitely one of them.

D: How has this knowledge, awareness, and perspective affected your relationship with your parents?

V: The way it works for me is as I was growing, this grew with me. So, part of my growing process was going though these sessions, or going through this awareness. So, as they've seen me grow and mature as a person, or academically or physically, they've seen this occur as well. My mother can just sit back and think that it's really great and that I'm incredible or something like that. And my father, it's hard, because I look at him and I feel past him sometimes and that doesn't always feel right because I'm so used to his being the one, the expert; so smart, so knowledgeable.

D: Just like the yielding to the machine. When you looked at your machine is it more of your father's machine or your mother's machine?

V: Probably father's.

D: Has your ability to show up center stage, affected your relationship with them? In other words, has it drawn them out from the sidelines a little more, or is it, in some way, what we talked about earlier, a trigger or a threat to their machine?

V: I think sometimes, it's both. If I read them something, or if they see me doing something, they'll be very touched. I can read them my journal from my trip; they'll get big tears in their eyes. And other times, it is more of a threat. I also know that if I'm real, my father will be real. I don't know if it's because he and I maybe have similar machines that we engage so easily and are able to miss each other's real selves a lot easier then engage and trigger each other. I think we trigger each other more than we engage our real selves. Definitely. It's really easy to say it's just my dad, he doesn't know, oh well, big loss. But you have to stop and say what am I doing. Why am I not being as real as I could be around him, because I know that if I'm real, he's real? So, it he's not being real, I must not be being real either, so I have a responsibility. I think a lot of that involves the fact that I still do, even though I know he loves me and I know I am important to him. I do not always feel that way. When I do share my feelings, I do not feel they're always valued. I feel sometimes they are downplayed as being trivial. Things in my life that have happened that my mother loves hearing about, or is interested in or that I want to talk about aren't seen that way. So, I think there's that reluctance to share that if it's not going to be valued or if it's not going to be recognized. It all comes back to you.

D: How about in relationships with people your age. Any comment you want to make there?

V: They think I'm an angel. They see what I do with other people or they watch me, or see how I feel what they feel. When I'm being me with them, I think it touches them. And especially if I'm younger than they are, that's their rationalization, "Oh, Veronica, she's just some little angel from California." It's sweet, but it's like she's different than we are, she's special. Not that they have it in them too. I feel it is appreciated at school and in situations where people are upset, but it also gets hard to say "No, I need to sleep or I need to do this for myself." When you see a great need you want to keep giving to it, but with my peers, it's helped the way you communicate with each other or the way you talk to each other. In regards to my peers, I think, I'm nothing but good things in terms of relationships, confrontations, the way we can explain things to each other, the way we talk. And then, there are those people that I think it's too much for and that's real hard. When it's too much for them and it overwhelms them, they leave.

D: Those are the people you are referring to as it threatens, even though you are not trying to hurt them.

V: Or it's just like, "Who's this girl? Where did she come from?" Or if I say something to someone and they say, "Are you a witch? How did you know that?" I just know. "How do you see these things in me? How did you know this?" And I'm not doing it like, "I found you out." It's not like that, but that's uneasy when they think that no one can see it and some do. I guess it's pretty shocking.

D: To the machine it is. Because you said earlier that you, the real self, was delighted or pleased and the machine was shocked. And the machine was shocked because if we can see you, we can hurt you. You're delighted because, if you can see me, I must be there, if you can see me, maybe I'll come out, if you can see me; you might like me. If you can see me, maybe I can come out and play?

HAVING THE MACHINE WORK FOR YOU

In this book, I have tried to show you through the use of many metaphors and the simple model that I've created, a way of looking into the human psyche and a way of understanding yourself with a particular emphasis on why your mind lies to you. I'd like to now focus on how you can get your mind to work for you. Now of course its' worked for you in its' own automatic way, hence the word machine. It automatically comes on, it automatically decides what's dangerous or not, it automatically has a built-in coping mechanism, as we've learned, but to work on yourself and make a new choice, and a new set of choices about your mind is the true way of achieving what I've called personal balance tm. Personal balance is a state of mind or consciousness where the authentic is now sitting in the front seat driving the car, and the machine is in the passengers' seat. I've used the metaphor of the car in previous chapters to show how the machine is constantly in control. Now, of course, we've allowed this to happen because our mind is protecting us and we, of course, have not wanted to feel any more fear or pain, so we slowly slip into the back seat, and as mentioned earlier, if the trauma is so great in our lives, the machine puts us in the trunk for greater safety, and if the trauma was severe enough, we're placed outside the car in a U Haul. Most people are in the back seat, safe and sound as indicated earlier with the tinted windows so that no one can see in, but we can see out. I've liked to use the metaphor of what I call the teddy bear and the tank. A big tank is going down the street with its' turret and gun focusing on certain things all masterminded by the machine, we the teddy bear, are sitting inside of the tank safe and sound, however, people that walk by see the tank and are frightened immediately of it. Our machine, of course, has evidence to say that these peoples' reactions which are fearful, confused, and reluctant to interact with us are signs of danger. People are merely **responding to our tank**. They can't see us. If we pulled the tank up and rolled one of the windows down and they got to see our authentic, the simple beauty of our vulnerable self, they would be immediately disarmed, and of course, want to interact with us because there's no danger. However, what they see and hear is the clanking of this tank down the street and, of course, they assume a more defensive posture in response to it. Our machine then has the evidence to tell us that people are not safe because they look at us defensively, resistively, and fearfully. What's actually happening is they're responding to us in our defensive posture (the tank). We, of course, continue to get the evidence through our machine that they are dangerous, and therefore, it's not safe to come out. So, it's a never ending continuation of fear and doubt that bombard us on a daily basis.

There's a metaphor I like to use about remaining in the present and staying in tune with the present and *not* being influenced by the continuous autonomy of that mega machine; our mind. The cable cars in San Francisco are propelled by a cable that runs underground. There is a factory with turbines that generate this very thick cable that moves at a constant speed under the ground. The cable cars merely attach themselves to it to propel themselves and the drivers of the cars disengage that attachment and put the brakes on in order to stop. The cable to me represents the constant flow of energy which comes from a greater Source. I am giving you my opinion here, so I believe that the constant flow of energy that which comes from the Source is coming from God. God is the cable flow of energy, an underlying deep flow of power that runs beneath our existence. The mind, of course, does not believe in God, the mind wants proof. As mentioned earlier in this book, the mind wants to see and understand God, the authentic feels God's existence. The mind wants proof that God exists; but the authentic just "knows" that God exists. When one is in the present, when one can get to the present, when one can overtake the mind and prevent it from using its' binoculars or looking into the rear view mirror, when one can make *the choice* one can be in the present. Once in the present, there is an immediate engagement and attachment to the cable. When connected to the cable, you can feel the flow of that source of energy, and if you can practice staying attached to it, you can get the benefits of that attachment.

I invite you to create an intention. An intention is a thought, a seed, a picture or vision, of what you want, especially if it's out of contribution. I believe that an authentic intention when attached to the cable will create a powerful synergy and interaction which can cause incredible manifestations towards that vision planted by the intention. What I am saying here is quite simple. It's simple, yet it's very difficult to explain why and how it happens. In 1929, Zig Ziegler spoke of the power of positive thinking, there have been many people who have spoken or made reference to intention and positive thinking, and staying in the flow, and staying in the present, etc. The intention that is created by the authentic must never be from a greedy place, or a place of wanting. The intention must be out of contribution. Let me tell you a few stories in my own life of how I've used the power of intention and the attachment to the cable to help me get there to show you how things can be manifested and brought forth from the universe to help you fulfill your dream. Now I caution you, that there are many machine thinking people that would consider this to be somewhat edgy, fringy, even" hee- be- gee- be" type thinking, because it's difficult to prove how it happens, but I assure you from my heart, that it *does* happen. Years ago, I worked at a center for the developmentally disabled. In this center, there was a number of programs to help these developmentally disabled people with various occupations. For example, there was a factory where they actually made different products and built things like skateboards and a variety of items. They had a horticulture program, a food service program, and a janitorial program in this center. I was playing chess one day with one of the students there, his name was Andrew. Andrew was about thirty years old, lived with his mother, was an extremely quiet and passive guy who had cognitive impairment due to his developmental disability, however, he could beat me at chess and I play a fairly good game of chess. It was amazing to me that he was able to use his left hemisphere so well because that's the analytical part of us that's the logical, sequential processing of information part of us that is extremely critical to use, especially to decide the strategy of a chess game. Yet, socially, he was very withdrawn and passive, had a lot of anxiety, and was very quiet with very flat affect in his mood. He would, however, give a little bit of a smirk when he was able to beat Dr. French in another chess game. One of the parents at the center (who actually later became my father in law), worked at IBM, so I had an idea that Andrew, because of his ability to process things with his left hemisphere, could actually learn how to run or use a computer. I immediately contacted Mr. Richard Howell and he was able to set up a meeting with me and Andrew. After I obtained permission from Andrew's mother, we went to IBM and an instructor there showed Andrew a System 32 computer. This was many years ago, in the late seventies when this occurred. Computers at that time were very big and bulky and were not like the unbelievable laptops, Ipods, Ipads, etc., that we see today. When Andrew was shown the System 32 computer the instructor showed him the various ways it worked, how to turn it on, how to use it, etc. I videotaped the interaction of Andrew's learning, and I made a presentation to IBM. IBM was so impressed with Andrew's ability to actually control and fulfill the learning requirements for this computer, that they donated a trailer and ten computers, and even a teacher! The teacher that taught Andrew that day took a sabbatical leave from IBM because she was so excited about the possibility of teaching other developmentally disabled adults the use of a computer. In that first class, I was standing in the trailer watching the teacher teach the ten students, Andrew was of course one of them, and I was touched by a moment of what I call bliss and joy. I had gone full circle on having an intention to have the nation's first computer operator program for the developmentally disabled come to fruition. I was emotionally touched by seeing Andrew in the class and knew that the intention had actually occurred. Intention is a way of crystallizing a thought into reality. As I said earlier, the intention must be one that is not driven by greed. If the intention is honorable and is out of contribution to good, to provide service to others, that intention, when fueled by continual faith and belief, can begin to grow as a seed from the source of our energy. Our authentic, which I said earlier, is connected to God, remains attached to the cable. The attachment to the cable causes a flow of energy that will guide the authentic. Without the use of the machine and all of its' fancy global satellite systems, it's being guided by a deeper place. It's having a strong belief. The belief we have in God is fueled by our faith, that same faith is used in the belief of the intention. I would visualize Andrew being in that class. I would visualize some sort of teacher there, some sort of surroundings with having the computers there, I was making my own authentic movie. Now this movie is fueled and fed by a constant visualization and emotional belief in the movie. When I was a child, my father would tell me, if you want to play baseball and be really good at it, you've got to eat, sleep, and drink baseball. There were times I would sleep in my uniform so I could wake up for the game. It's a similar kind of belief. One has to eat, sleep, and drink the intention. How is this done? It's done by clearly having a picture of what you want, and again, *it cannot be out of greed.* You can't think I want to have a million dollars, or I want to own this big car or this big house, those are materialistic possessions. They have to be intentions that are fueled by a sense of contribution, so any moments I had, that I had to myself, whether they be in the shower, in the bathroom, driving my car, at a red light, in between patients, I would visualize, I would see and feed the movie; by seeing it over and over, by remembering what it looked like, by feeding the emotional part of the movie, by watching all the people in the movie, it begins to give it life. This intention, which is an authentic movie, is the beginning of how dreams can come true. The movie's existing and being continually fed by moments in time when there are no distractions. The movie is believed through the same faith that we believe in God. We surrender the movie to God, or to the source of energy, and we allow ourselves to be engaged by the cable. The cable guides us into opportunities where things will show up from the universe to help manifest that dream. Things would happen like the parent that worked at IBM happened to be at that center. The parent arranged my visit with Andrew at IBM. IBM allowed the teacher that happened to be that same teacher with Andrew take the sabbatical, etc. I know you get the idea. Now some people would hear that and say that I was lucky or it was coincidental that IBM did that. I know differently. There are many other stories that are like this, but I wanted to give you some examples of how an authentic intention can manifest itself into a dream, and how that dream can crystallize into reality.

In my office in Whittier, I had an idea of setting up a Mental Health Center for Senior Citizens. I worked for CareMore, which is a very large medical management company who provides services for Medicare and senior citizens. CareMore is a leader in providing services for senior citizens. I had set up the first Mental Health Center in Long Beach several years prior and I wanted to set up another Mental Health Center in Whittier. The office next to mine, which was in a brand new building, was completely bare, only plywood. In between patients, I would walk next door and I would walk around that plywood and imagine where the waiting room was, where my office would be, where the break room was, where the psychiatrist's office would be, the group room, and all the other therapist's offices. Once again, I was fueling the intention. By physically walking around the room I could get a feel for everything and I continued to help feed the movie. Now fast forward to where it was built and functioning. One day, as we had just opened our doors, I walked into the waiting room and saw eight or ten patients there with their wheelchairs, oxygen tanks, and the like, waiting to be seen for mental health services. One of the patients had given one of the receptionists a warm plate of cookies that she'd baked because she was so happy to come to this mental health center. These two centers are the first of their kind anywhere. We provide on-going treatment for CareMores' patients. We assess for dementia, alzheimers, and provide medication. We provide bilingual/bicultural staff services and individual group psychotherapy services. It's a very successful program, and I am very proud of my association with CareMore and their ability to have the vision that connected with my vision. I appreciate the opportunity to toot my horn here about this program and about the other program because I am very proud of these accomplishments. In fact, to give you a brief update, the program that was set up at that center (The San Gabriel Valley Training Center), now graduates thirty to forty graduates per year and has been going on ever since 1976. Andrew left the center and got a job working for a business sending out invoices making about 1,500 to 1,800 dollars a month. This was a lot different than the few dollars he made making skateboards and working on the assembly line in that factory. Today at CareMore, our Mental Health Center services 700-800 patients per month for a variety of mental health benefits.

An intention is an extremely powerful opportunity for the authentic to create. We were created by God, the ultimate Creator, and we are given the opportunity to create. Creations can also occur by the machine. The machine can be very successful and the machine can make a lot of money, the machine can do a lot of things because it's driven. Many of the successful people in our country who are mostly machines have become successful in their own right, but, to be successful authentically is to be more balanced with contribution, not greed. To be successful authentically is to be balanced spiritually, emotionally, psychologically, and physically. To me a successful person puts their family first, puts their relationship with God first, and has a career that is out of contribution and love. I absolutely love what I do. I've been doing it for thirty years. I don't look at Monday's like another dreaded day that I have to go back to work. The times I get triggered in my practice is having to wait for money or collect money from insurance companies, and so on. I do hire someone for that service but that is what triggers me. When I shut the doors to my office, and I'm in there with a patient, I feel I am doing God's work. I am doing the work I am supposed to do out of my gift; my gift of contribution. If you follow your gift, and you use it with passion, the money will follow. I don't do things out of money first, I do things out of contribution first. What I am inviting you to do is just begin to visualize what you want out of contribution, and use the gifts God gave you to help bring that contribution to life. By doing this, you will be able to realize the ultimate dream of watching your authentic intention crystallize into reality. Now, there is something that happens during this crystallization process that still intrigues me today, I can't explain it to you because your machine and other machines want an explanation, I can only tell you through my experience that it works. What I can't explain is how the universe will provide information and assistance at times when it would seem unlikely. Things will happen in the course of your visualization that will appear to other people as coincidental or lucky as I said earlier, however, you'll know secretly that it's from the manifestation of your intention.

Recently, Wayne Dyer has written several books on this power of intention. Daniel Amens book on *"Change Your Thoughts, Change Your Life,"* both focus on what I'm speaking to you about now. A short time ago I gave a lecture to a group of salespeople and I was telling them about how to make a "connection." I spoke of "sharing" versus "selling." The metaphor I use is a picture of a piece of string. If you put the piece of string on the table you can't push the string, in other words, you can't force things. When we feel like we are operating out of scarcity or fear, the machine pushes forward to push that string to **make something happen**. The trick is to **stay in faith** and **believe** we're already in abundance. At this lecture, a young woman mentioned "Dr. French, I think all you have to do is make a choice and tell your mind to stop thinking negatively, and just control the way it thinks." I told her I knew that was easy for her because she's come to a place where she could have that kind of empowerment but for most people this is very difficult. But she said for her, she was able to do it because she realized that all the things that she'd done prior to that (the things her machine had done) had not worked. It was clear to me that this woman had gone through her own pain, opened that closet door to some degree and worked through the pain, and got to the place where she reestablished and reclaimed herself by getting in that drivers' seat. (being more in the present). When you choose to not listen to your mind, when you choose to believe what you want to believe and not believe the lies of the mind, you are reclaiming yourself. When you realize that what your mind has been doing is just to keep you automatically surviving and you are not living your life, you've just survived it, then you might begin to see that moving to the front seat is a better deal. You see, no one could hurt you like you hurt you. The expression "we are a prisoner of our own mind" has been around for a thousand years. Here's another expression, "we create that which we are afraid of." If you think of something long enough, if you allow your mind to be fearful enough, the manifestation that I spoke of earlier, will happen in a negative way. If the mind stays in fear and doubt, and you start expecting something bad is going to happen, and you continually worry about that bad thing happening, I promise, on some level, **you will draw it towards you.** We do create that which we are afraid of, but we can also create that which we have good intentions for, it's all up to you, it's your choice. Do you want the machine running you, keeping you in the back seat, safe, or do you want to be responsible for your own life and your own happiness and reclaim and take charge of yourself? Most people go along with the ride because they don't think that they can do anything about it. I'll admit, it's not easy to stay in abundance when things are scary and scarce around you. It's not easy to stay in faith, when all the crocodiles have a hold on you as I mentioned in the earlier chapter, but, if you can stay focused and believe that you are protected, not by your machine, but by a much deeper source of energy which I call God, then you can surrender to that source, get out of your own head, drop down into where your true strength really is. Your true strength exists, not in your mind, or by your mind, it exists in an emotional state that you always had when you were little. When you were younger, you already had the state, you just didn't know it. When you became eight or ten and the beginning of the mask formed, that's when you left yourself, I am sorry that all of us were hurt, all of us fell as children, some of us fell on our heads, some of us were more damaged, but let's stop feeling sorry for ourselves and stop pitying ourselves. Let's stop the negativity and the fear and doubt, and go forward with a new plan. When you stay inside of yourself year after year, you are buried alive. The mind which has taken care of you all those years without knowing it, has actually contributed to helping you suffocate. Think of it that way. Think of a mother holding her baby so tight because she doesn't want anything to hurt it, that she's actually cutting off its' oxygen. How do you tell that mother that she doesn't love her baby. She loves her baby with everything inside of her, but she doesn't realize that squeezing so hard is causing suffocation. The mind doesn't realize that by keeping us inside safe, hidden from view, it's actually hurting us. The mind doesn't realize that all the interpretations that it has, all the second guessing that it's doing, is futile. None of it is true. No one is really trying to hurt us. As I mentioned before, unless they have a knife or a gun or there's a right hook coming at you, or there's a fire, flood, earthquake, or some other disaster, or there's a car accident, or something's going to fall on you or it's a ball flying at you, or something is going to hit you, nothing is really dangerous other than that. Every other human interaction that you have, all interpersonal reactions that you have where you get your feelings hurt, all of that is a lie as interpreted by your mind. By you staying in belief, by you staying clear, and staying focused on an intention of contribution, by you remaining in a place where you can feed that movie, through your constant eating, sleeping, and drinking it, you will be part of an incredible process of creating for the Creator. You will make a contribution to the planet that will serve others and you will have rewards of that contribution, because as I said, acting out of your passion and out of your gifts comes *first* and then the money will follow.

All of this is based on faith, faith in yourself, and faith in God, faith in the source and faith in the energy of that cable that exists down underneath. You can't grab the cable if you have any fear or doubt. Once you surrender and you leave the attic of your mind and you come downstairs to where you truly live, you will feel the presence of that cable. Children know it, and babies are absolutely still connected to it. Babies who are just here for a few days or a few weeks come with the radiant energy of that connection, that's why we are so attracted to babies because they are vulnerable; and they are radiantly authentic. They know something that we don't know, but they can't tell us what they know because they don't know what they know. That's a very high state. To not know what you don't know. You see, the mind wants to know everything and we think if we could know something then we must understand it because faith is too vague, it's too scary, it's too foggy, it's not clear. Faith is accepting something that you can't see, the mind doesn't like any of this. Remember, it's got the high powered binoculars, it's got high powered microscopes, it's got global satellite interpretations, if it can't analyze it or catch it on the radar screen, then it must not exist. But to slip down into a deeper recess, to go down into a quieter place, to remember what you felt like when you were seven again, and to take that vulnerability into the outside and not allow the interpretations of the mind to distract you, now you have something to work with. You get a chance to be reborn, and get a chance to reclaim yourself because no one can hurt you like you have already hurt you. That hit me one day in a very big way. You know the metaphor we use when a light bulb comes on and you "get it." When I had this realization, it was like the whole stadium lit up when I "got it." I realized that I am public enemy number one! I am the one that knows how to hurt me, I am the one that keeps me harbored inside, I am the one that allows my machine to drive, I'm the one that stays passively in the back seat watching my machine take care of me when months turn into years and years turn into a lifetime. I got tired of that because I realized what was working, and what was not working. I got tired of that because I felt "better" being more authentic, yes, it's riskier, yes, I'm more vulnerable, yes, I'm even more defensive. I am more defensive because I am more exposed. I feel myself getting defensive because I can feel myself in my own vulnerability, but I know, at least, where I am, and I take full responsibility for it. The work is to stay in faith and to keep the distractions of doubt and fear away. The work is to decide what contribution to do next in order to serve God and the planet and my fellow brothers and sisters. The work is to take the gifts that I have been given by God and use them in a place of contribution. The work is to believe against all the odds and all the distractions that by surrendering and letting go and by not trying I can connect to the cable, I find the cable by letting go. You do not find the cable by trying to find the cable. Once I'm attached to the cable, the cable takes me to where I am supposed to go and the intention I have is the map and basis for the dream that will eventually come through. I get to experience the dream first hand. I visualized it and you will visualize yours. I'm inviting you to take this adventure. I'm inviting you to do the work on yourself and reclaim yourself and be empowered again. To feel alive is to feel life; to stay in fear and doubt is to survive and not move. Come on out and play – look for me, I'm out there on my bike riding up and down the street looking for someone to play with.

NOTES TO MYSELF: PART 1

When it comes to risking we all want the "absolute guarantee" we all want to be able to know that's it's absolutely safe where there is no danger or no pain. The truth is, we're all afraid of going first. But a fascinating thing happens when you do go first. If you risk first, it will call to the authentic part of someone else to come out and play. If you remain your machine first, you will call to the machine in the other person to join you. One calls to the other. In other words, if we are willing to surrender, in blind faith, our own vulnerability, then we will call to the vulnerability and the person that we are surrendering to. The machine has various coping mechanisms as I've described earlier. The machine picks "distractions" that are proportional to the amount of pain that it is trying to cover up. The more intense the distraction, the more intense the pain is that the machine is trying to cover. It keeps you from feeling something that is very threatening to the machine. Next time you catch yourself thinking about something, ask yourself, "If I wasn't thinking right now, what would I really be feeling?"

The machine has to think, but my authentic just **knows.** The machine thinks that it feels, but my authentic really and truly feels. God is the soul of the authentic self. God is part of the collective unconscious of all the authentic selves at the same time and in the same moment. Jesus Christ had no machine. He was purely and absolutely authentic at every moment. Because of this fluidity he had direct empowerment from God the father. My interpretation of what Christ said while on the cross "Forgive them father, for they know not what they do" is "Forgive their machines father, for they know not what they are doing."

Real time is the moment by moment fluid expression of the authentic self.

If I think that someone is the problem, then I know the problem is really me.

Whenever I justify or explain myself or blame others, then I am already being my machine.

My machine analyzes; my authentic feels. My machine decides and reacts; but my authentic chooses.

When I am not trusting myself I take what the machine interprets to be dangerous as a fact, rather than feeling it for myself or risking the experience for myself. When I'm in that place, I must bounce off my machine first because I am not able to show up authentically and experience the situation directly. If I do get it directly and tell my machine to back off and I experience some form of hurt or injury, then my machine beats me up on the inside, lectures me, and continues to tell me that I made a mistake and that next time it will ensure my protection.

My machine won't allow me to get too happy because it believes I will then get too hurt and then it will get angry with me for being so stupid.

If I allow someone in to see the real me, and somehow I experience hurt or injury and I handle it without the machine, the machine tries to punish me because it wants things to go back to the way they were. It wants me to go inside so that it can stay out there in the interest of protecting me.

My authentic intentions are always good and honorable; but it's my machine's delivery that continues to get misperceived.

When I'm in a bad place with myself I take your machine personally. When I 'm in an authentic, loving place, I look past your machine and see the real you. I can forgive your machine and embrace your authentic when I'm in a loving place.

The only way I can "know" you is after I "know" me.

When I'm in a loving authentic place, I can see your machine for what it does *for you* instead of what it does *to me*. In other words, I can see how it serves you, rather than taking it personally.

It's no fun being grown up, but it's fun growing up.

The authentic self is like a flower that is in each and every one of us. Someday soon we will all blossom together and experience an eternal springtime.

I learned to give, when I learned how to accept.

When I start forgetting who I am, I stop for a moment and try to feel myself to remember.

Sleeping is yet another state of awareness.

When I talk, I listen to you, and hear me. You are a reflection of my innermost being, because we are made of the same fabric.

Animals have great wisdom in their eyes.

In regards to the issue of time, when my machine thinks about it, time exists. When I am authentic and I feel about it, I am eternal. Living in the past or living in the future does not enrich my growth. Living "now" is a much healthier arrangement.

Hostility results when I have not gotten my feelings out at the time that they were felt.

I don't like to work; I like to play. My work is my play.

In sixty two years I have found out that the more I discover about myself , the more I know how little I really know.

Death does not exist when I am feeling my life – only life around me is experienced.

My struggling in becoming authentic is to be complete, completely aware of who I am.

When I think about doing something I'm analyzing life. When I do what I'm feeling about something, I'm living my life.

To live yesterday is to remember, to live tomorrow is to forget, to live today is to know. What happened yesterday is past, what will happen tomorrow remains to be experienced, and what happens now is truly what I struggle with.

Words are one way to communicate, yet when I touch someone or I am touched, a complete understanding is felt.

The feeling I have had in meeting some people for the very first time is one of recognizing and old friend.

When I question things, it's because I have forgotten who I am. When I accept things it is because I am remembering.

To get the complete picture, I must be completely in the picture, otherwise I am fragmented.

When I play I am spontaneously full of energy. When I work I am driven and I tire easily. To learn to play at work is the secret.

Home is where my friends are. When I'm lost I go home to a friend and then I know where I am.

The exchange of love between my mother and father gave me life. The exchange of life that I share with others gives me love.

The greatest teachers that I've ever had never taught me but only guided me into teaching myself.

The space between two people who are being authentic is full of radiant energy but the space between two people who are being their machines is just space.

The secret of loving is surrendering.

When I expect something I get nothing. When I expect nothing I get something.

When I go into a new situation sometimes I go into it and I'm in a triggered state. In this triggered state, my mind films the situation and takes copious notes to help reduce the uncertainty; so when I think that I'm the machine, and I'm denying my real self, then I take the machine's notes and the film as "the real experience."

Once we have experienced early pain as a child, our mind is there to take care of us. It escorts us into a secret room to ensure our protection. How clever this is. If you forget where you are, no one else will be able to find you either, they won't be able to hurt you, and you also won't have to be reminded of what hurt you in the past. Here is the special room where you can stay safe and free from harm, in fact, in this privacy vault, you can hide what bothers you long enough to forget it; the only problem is that you begin burying yourself alive.

In reviewing all the ways that people could hurt me through rejection, criticism, shaming, humiliation, etc., I decided that the one person who would be able to hurt me the most is actually me. I know everything about me, I know more about the way I really am, I know all of my internal buttons and triggers; the truth is, if I have to worry about someone really hurting me, I'm the only one that really knows how to hurt me the most. I'm actually public enemy number one. *It's not any of you after all!*

True happiness can never be achieved until you give yourself permission to be the person that God made you to be, to be your authentic self.

Out of all the comforts provided by the material world, and by our need to seek pleasure and avoid pain, the most important reason, the one which makes all of this possible is not provided, that is in being comfortable with yourself.

It's important to spend time by yourself. The average person could not go and sit inside their home shutting off all lights and all distractions, all music, phones, TV's, Blackberry's, IPod's, etc., to sit quietly in the dark and listen to the sound of their own breathing because it frightens them. It's because when we remove all those distractions a person is profoundly reminded of the closet door of pain that they secretly hold inside which harbors all of their hurt and anger. To be aware of this without distraction is a frightening experience.

When you answer the phone, try answering with a little smile in your voice, I promise you the other person can hear it.

When giving something, try to make sure that you're not looking for the thank you. The best giving is done anonymously. Give people more than they expect, you will be pleasantly surprised at the outcome. Once you realize you've made a mistake, take steps right away to correct it, even though it's uncomfortable. It's important to take responsibility for what you've done. Your machine will tell you that people will think less of you, be critical of you, and so on. The truth is, people will respect you and it will give them permission and remind them that they too can do the same when they've made a mistake. Be happy for someone else's success. The reason why many of us are unhappy is because we are being reminded that someone else is taking risks that we're too afraid to take. Whenever you are able to say you are sorry, try to say it from an authentic place, especially looking someone in their eyes when you're saying it.

Compassion is moment by moment listening.

If I want the real you to come out, it's absolutely essential for me to risk being authentic *first.*

Mercy is undeserved forgiveness.

Guilt is unexpressed resentment or when our anger is turned inward. In my work on myself I have made an interesting discovery. I've learned that I have a need to make you okay. If I see you and you are not in a good place, or in some way you are uncomfortable, I'm immediately triggered and want to connect with you. On the surface, it appears as though I am genuinely interested in you. But as I've discovered my need to "connect with you" is self serving. This is not my proudest moment to admit this, but when I make you okay, and put you at ease, it helps me be okay, and puts me at ease. So I need to confess, I'm not just doing it because I care about you,

I'm doing it because I need to take care of me. This is another subtle way that my machine acts and actually sounds authentic. Years ago, I was opening the mail with one of my secretaries. She had been a secretary of mine for several years, and I was quite fond of her. I noticed that she seemed to be a bit preoccupied, or pensive, so I asked her if she was okay, and she answered, "of course." A few minutes later, I asked again and said, "Are you sure you're okay?" And she reassured me that she was. A few minutes later, I said, "You know, I care about you, and if it's something personal and you don't want to discuss it I respect that, but I sense that there's something bothering you." She turned to me and looked at me in the eyes and said "Maybe something's bothering you!" Well, this of course, surprised and fascinated me. I immediately took stock of where I was at that moment emotionally and realized that I had that need to make her okay, as I've just mentioned. I said to her, there's something very important I want to ask you and that is "What did you feel when I said to you that I cared about you?" She said, "That's interesting, because I know that you do care, but at the moment that you said that, I didn't feel it." This is another indication of how my machine **sounded** authentic and actually said an authentic truth about my caring about her, but it was, indeed, manipulative because it was used for me to feel better. This is how subtle the mind can be in helping us cope with our discomfort.

In the past it was easy for me to look at your machine and have definite reasons why I should not risk or be at ease, or feel safe, because when your machine was on, it felt legitimately justifiable not to risk the authentic part of me. What I've learned today is that when your machine is on, it's because you're in trouble, and my work is not to take that personally. In fact, I must treat you better than you deserve to be treated. Indeed this is when you **need me the most.** It's easy to be around someone when there's a joyful, lighthearted moment. But when you are drowning emotionally, that's when you need me the most and it is when you look the most dangerous. I must talk to the real you, even though I can't see you. I must risk in the presence of your machine, even though I can't feel or see you. Of course, in doing this, my machine is screaming at me on the inside like a parent who is watching its child run across the freeway. It thinks I am crazy for wanting to place myself in the midst of this danger, when I 'm not armed. It would tell me that I'm going to be shredded and disintegrate. It would cry out to me urging me to get inside, because it did not sense one degree of safety out there. But in taking that risk and remaining authentic in the presence of your machine, I found out that the teeth of your machine were actually made of rubber, and that there was, in fact, no danger at all. In fact, when I took that risk, I had immediate access to the authentic part of you. I was able to find where you lived without any danger or risk to me. Showing you mercy is forgiving you when you don't deserve it. This is the road to real intimacy. This is the state of grace. This is what our work as human beings truly is.

I have an interesting metaphor to share with you. When your machine is going off, it's just like you are drowning. If I swim over to you to try to help you, and you slap me in the face, my machine has evidence that you hurt me. When I swim ashore and tell the lifeguard about how you hit me and show him my bloody nose, the lifeguard remarks, "But you're standing on the sand here, and that other person out there is drowning!" Of course, I do get some sympathy and attention from the lifeguard because I have evidence of blood, but the truth is that the drowning person was not intending to harm me in any way. The only issue for them is their survival. Did they scratch my skin and draw blood from me? Yes. Did they try to hurt me? No. Did I feel pain? Yes. Was my pain real? Yes. Was anyone maliciously trying to harm me? No. My real work here is to show compassion for the person who hit me and forgive them because they were not trying to hurt me, merely trying to save themselves. If that person was wearing a sign around their neck, and it told me of all the pain that they'd been in, or if I could see the movie of their life and knew all the pain that they went through as a child, it would allow me a micro second of compassion and another perspective so as to not get caught up in my own injury and my pain. It allows me to show mercy, and be compassionate. When I am able to show up authentically, it disarms their machine and calls to their authentic to come out.

Several years ago, I was in a restaurant and went to pay the bill and I needed to borrow a pen. I asked the cashier, "Excuse me, do you happen to have a pen I could borrow?" The cashier snapped back, "I don't know where the hell any pens are!" I immediately felt the slap on my face, and felt I didn't deserve to be treated like that. Of course, at that moment, I knew I was triggered. Obviously, this person was in an awful place of pain and I was able to have a perspective that this person was drowning. I thought to myself, maybe this is his last day on the job, and he has four children. Maybe his little girl was hit by a car and is in a coma in ICU. If this man was wearing a sign around their neck and it said, my wife has cancer and I just found out last night, and it's terminal, we have four young children and I'm terrified. I would have read that sign and he could have said anything to me, snapped at me, and yelled at me, and out of compassion, I would have forgiven him and maybe even asked to take over his shift while he went to the hospital to be with his wife. The problem is none of us are wearing signs, so none of us know of each other's history. We just keep taking each other's machines personally.

Throughout my life, my machine has accumulated files on all of you and has remarked about your masks and the way that you've acted that I found to be rude and offensive and obnoxious. I've judged and categorized you. I've listened to my own machines lies about you and my machine has set up a belief system about all of you. I might even avoid you and find you offensive. Through the work that I've done on myself, and the model that I'm presenting to you now, I realize something extremely important; and that is, I am all of those things, that I accuse you of. I've always had an issue with people that are rude and insensitive who acted like bullies. Certainly I could justify this because of my early childhood experiences where bullies picked on me and the rude and insensitive people that I would encounter. I certainly had evidence because of the definite feeling of pain and the belief that I'd been injured. What I now realize and know, is that when I'm triggered, *I become the very insensitive bully that I can't stand in you!* When I look at all of this I realize you aren't doing anything to me; everything I've done, I've done to myself, my machine perceives you're hurting me, and that it is personal and that there is intent on your part to hurt me. But the truth is you're not trying to hurt me, remember, your drowning. If I take your drowning personally, I can add to my machines belief systems and strengthen what it thinks it knows to be true. When I show you mercy, in other words, that undeserved forgiveness, then I can look past the drowning and know that even though I can't read the sign around your neck, you have a history, and you have pain, and you're merely trying to survive. I don't have to take it personally. There is such a thing as genuine danger; fire, flood, car accidents, a knife, a gun, etc. But all the other things that happen interpersonally between people; all the other triggers that we experience socially, *all of these triggers are lies*. No one is really trying to hurt us; no one is trying to do anything to us. The Psychiatrist/Minister, M. Scott Peck pointed out in one of his books "life is not easy, life is not fair, pain is inevitable, suffering is optional." The only thing you have control over is the amount of suffering or pain that you are experiencing. You have no control over what's happening to your children right now, or your spouse or a loved one. You can't control what I'm thinking right now, or what

I am going to say next. You can't control anything else in the world. The only thing you have control over are your own feelings; and those feelings are being carefully monitored and guarded by a very dominant part of you, your twin brother, your twin sister, your machine.

NOTES TO MYSELF: PART 2

When two people meet each other for the very first time it is important for each one to feel approved and liked. Because of that need to be accepted neither person wants to "risk or go first." What usually happens is a subtle dance and exchange so as to "feel each other out" with the understanding that the goal is to be liked and loved. Each time that we feel an injury or feel that someone has hurt us we record it and believe that a "piece of us" has been damaged and injured and that somehow we now are left with **less** of us. We go on to believe that the more we get injured or hurt that the self that we have will continue to reduce in size until we are left with only a small piece or fragment that then must be housed deep within our psyche so as to protect us from total disintegration. People actually believe this and so there is a point of no return where one has had enough emotional damage that one decides that it cannot risk unless there is "absolute certainty" that there will be no possibility of any further injury. Psychiatrists call this fear "ego death" the total disintegration of the self. This notion *is a lie*. The truth, as I have experienced it, is that once I decided to risk the remains of myself after a long history of damage in my childhood and adulthood that absolutely nothing happened. Even if I believed that I was injured once again I did not lose the last fragment. In fact what I discovered is that there is a ***never ending supply*** of the real me. I lived for years with the belief, based upon the validation of many of my friends and associates, that there was only one self that I had and that each time it was injured it would reduce in size and capacity. The truth is there is a never ending supply of that self. Therefore, the risk taking can be unlimited. Think of the possibilities!

When I feel injured or damaged, when we have evidence that someone is hurting us he accompanying emotional and visceral response is very real. Because we "feel" hurt then we believe it to be true. It must be true because we are feeling the actual pain. It reminds me of when my children might injure themselves in the course of playing and what they're most concerned about is if they are bleeding. In other words, if it's bleeding they must be hurt, if they're not bleeding then it doesn't seem to be that bad of an injury. We operate along the same line-if we have the emotional feeling, the gut feeling of experiencing hurt, then indeed we must have been hurt. For me to suggest to you that you are only "perceiving" the damage and that your machine only "thought" that there was damage when you are experiencing genuine emotional pain you would discount me in that belief immediately. You would try to defend the fact that the pain that you are feeling is "real." How can it be possible that your machine is lying to you when in fact you are feeling the realness of the pain. The answer is very simple: the pain you are feeling is a representation of the original pain that you had felt earlier in your life. The original pain called for the consultation of the machine hence the protection. Once the association was made the machine basically let you know that it would "watch out for you." So, you went along with your business and anything in the environment that looked like it, seemed like it, smelled like it, tasted like it, sounded like it, acted like it or was it clearly caused the triggered response and further coping and surviving in order to protect its most valuable possession: you.

THINGS THAT BOTHER ME ABOUT YOU

Throughout my life I would continue to remark about some of you and your masks and ways that you acted that I found offensive, rude and obnoxious. I would have judged or categorized you. I would set up a belief system about you. I might even avoid you and find you offensive. Through the work that I've done on myself and the model that I am presenting to you now I realized something extremely important and it is that I am *all those things* that I accuse you of. I always had an issue with people who were insensitive, rude, or who acted like bullies. Certainly I would justify this because of the number of bullies who picked on me when I was a child and the number of rude and insensitive people that I would encounter. I certainly had evidence because of the definite feeling of pain and belief that I had been injured. When I realize the truth I know that I am the biggest bully I can be, the rudest and most insensitive person I can be, and all those things that I thought you were. When I took at all of this I realize that *you aren't doing anything to me.* Everything that I have done I've done to myself. My machine perceives that you are hurting me and that it is personal – that there is intent on your part to hurt me.

MY NEED TO MAKE YOU OKAY

When I see you and I see that you are not in a good place or that you are uncomfortable or you are feeling some pain I am immediately drawn to wanting to connect with you. Now, on the surface, it appears as though I am genuinely interested in you, but many times I discover that my need to "connect with you" and attend to you is also self serving. When I can make you okay and put you at ease it helps make me okay and put me at ease so I need to tell you that I am not doing it just because I care about you, I am doing it because I need to take care of me. Another subtle way my machine acts and sounds authentic.

SHOWING MERCY: UNDESERVED FORGIVENESS

In the past it was easy for me to look at your machine and have definite reasons why I should not risk or be at ease or feel safe because when your machine was going off it felt legitimate and justifiable not to expose the more vulnerable part of me. What I have learned today is that when your machine is going off it's because you're in trouble and my work is to not take that personally. I, in fact, must **treat you better than you deserve**. I must talk to the real you even though you can't see you. Of course, in doing this, my machine would think that I am crazy for wanting to place myself in the midst of danger when I am not armed. It would, in fact, be screaming and warning me while I walked forward into the mouth of the dragon. It would tell me that I am going to be shredded and disintegrate (ego death). It would cry out to me like an overprotective parent who could not help its young survive. But in taking that risk I found out that the teeth of the dragon were made of rubber and that there was **no danger at all.** In fact, when I took that risk I had immediate access to the real you. I was able to find where you lived without any danger or risk to me. Showing you mercy is forgiving you even when you don't deserve it. This is the road to intimacy. This is the state of grace.

YOUR MACHINE IS NOT TRYING TO HURT ME

There is a metaphor that has worked very well for me and I use it in the moment especially when I am feeling triggered or I am seeing the presence of your machine as it approaches me with an angry voice or a rude insensitive bullying manner (it sets off all of my past issues as a child). The metaphor that I used earlier is that I believe that when a person's machine is going off it is like a person who is drowning. Imagine a person drowning and they are thrashing about trying to stay afloat while gasping for air. Now, you swim over to that person to try to help them and as you reach out to them in a loving, kind way, they scratch your face because of their frantic attempt to stay alive. You swim back to a group of friends and they ask you what happened, and they see the blood dripping from your face. You point back at the other person's machine and say, "that person did that to me, can you believe this?" Of course, you get their sympathy and attention because it sure seems like you have a legitimate reason to protect yourself and avoid that person. After all, you have blood, and the scratches on your face; but take a look at one important aspect and that is, what is their intention? The person drowning was not intending to harm or hurt you in any way. In fact, "you" were not the issue to them at al! What was an issue for them was their survival. Did they scratch your skin and draw blood from you? Yes. Did they hurt you? No. Did you feel pain? Yes. Was the pain real? Yes. Was anyone maliciously trying to hurt you? No. Could you not show compassion for that person who scratched you and forgive them because they were not trying to hurt you, merely trying to save themselves. This metaphor works very well for me during certain moments when I am in the presence of someone's machine and I am massively triggered. It allows me to gain a microsecond of compassion and another perspective so as not to get caught up in what I perceive to be "blood dripping down my face." It allows me to show mercy and be compassionate. When I show up authentically, it disarms their machine and draws their authentic self out.

WEARING THE SIGN

I use a tool to assist me in staying in touch with my authenticity. Sometimes I'm more successful at using it than at other times, but I would like to share it with you. I pretend I am wearing a sign around my neck that tells the truth about who I am. It might say that I am someone who, if triggered, can be manipulative, insensitive, rude, a bully, self-serving, a brat, a jerk and an angry machine. Now I know this might seem sort of ridiculous, but just imagine if everybody was really *on* to what your issues were and what was going on with you. In a way you couldn't get away with anything. They could look at you and just "know." This does bring the human interaction to a very interesting place because this full disclosure does not allow for anything other than the real you to come out. Since everyone "knows," there can be no deception only an invitation to live authentically. Try it sometime.

CELEBRATE YOUR SADNESS

We are living in such a narcissistic society where we have defined winning and success as how much we have and how pretty we look. We have sadly lost touch with a lot of what has substance and what is real. In this context many of us are driven towards self gratification and immediate pleasure. We certainly want to avoid pain yet if one can surrender and feel pain with the same degree of passion and willingness, one can then be free of the pain and go through it. It takes a great deal of energy to hold feelings inside. In fact, the word emotion can be broken down as "e" (energy) and "motion" indicating energy in motion. It takes energy to hold energy in motion inside. . by yielding to pain and releasing it through celebrating our sadness, our hurt, our helplessness, our loneliness, etc., then we are free from it. It will not own us we will own it and be released from it.

THE SIX LEVELS OF AWARENESS: ACHIEVING PERSONAL BALANCE ™

Awareness level 1: Knowing the separateness of the real self and your machine. Being aware of the mask that you wear and knowing how you hide your real feelings and your authentic self.

Awareness level 2: The willful intent or desire to want to challenge the machine. A desire to confront the automatic way that you have survived your life.

Awareness level 3: The confrontation/interpretation where the real self declares and is motivated to identify those triggers that activate the machine. At this point you are aware of the pact that you have made with the machine to protect you. You are eager to restore a sense of harmony within yourself and allow yourself to own the machine rather than the machine owning you.

Awareness level 4: Represents daily moment by moment risking of the real self and the education and modification of the machine. There is a constant surveillance of the machine's activity and a willingness to ask others for feedback about one's authenticity or automatic behavior. You can stop the further triggering and coping behavior and allow yourself to feel the pain until the authentic self emerges.

Awareness level 5: Daily forgiveness of other's machines. Consistent risking with minimal emotional pain. There is a balance between the real self and the machine because the real self is **not** taking the other's machine personally. There has been an inter psychic shift – the authentic self is totally responsible for itself and it makes choices and lives life.

Awareness level 6: The state of grace. This is a moment by moment state of Personal Balance™ that allow for the fluidity of psychic harmony, spiritual fulfillment and enlightenment. This is the ultimate level that one must try to achieve. This is having a audience with God to set the stage for your next authentic intention.

Genetic Transfer - It might be years before the technology can assist us in proving what I believe to be true. I believe that there is a genetic transfer of information regarding the machine. It is transferred from parent to child. I have seen accounts both personally and professionally, from hundreds of patients regarding their children and the extraordinary differences that exist between them. Mothers continue to report subtle differences in pregnancies and that the eventual birth of the child and subsequent observable personality was indeed similar to the experience the mother felt during the course of her pregnancy. How is it that some children "come out" very much like a particular parent? I'm not just referring to a particular way of coping or surviving that can be observed early on before any significant cognitive modeling of the parent has occurred.

Parental modeling - There are obvious early environmental influences that impact and shape the child. We have all experienced disappointments, rejections, humiliations, abuse, etc., in the course of our childhood. Remember, there are no perfect parents. I believe we must forgive our parents because they, in fact, acted with good intention. However, they were driven by their machine and automatic behavior which in turn affected the way we viewed ourselves and the way we negotiated our machine following the moments of original pain. We certainly learn about how to cope and or survive from watching and feeling our parents live, or I might say survive life.

Original pain - There comes a time when we feel loss, separation, rejection, humiliation, abuse, etc., from our parents and or significant other people in our environment. We do not have the cognitive ability to "understand" what has happened to us. But we do know one important thing that is validated by our machine's perception of pain and that is that we have just been injured. This model continues to demonstrate that the "injury" was a perceived threat and not a genuine injury. However, we experience the pain, we believe it to be about us, and at that moment when our innocence has been violated, when our vulnerability has been impacted we "call upon" our machine to help protect us. I believe that the pact that we make with our machine at that moment is the beginning of the perpetual lie. We essentially lie to ourselves in making this pact because in some unconscious way we "know" that the calling of the machine for protection is not authentic. It is the beginning of us becoming "other" than ourselves. It is the lie that forms the basis of fueling the machine and it is the lie that forms the basis of our self deception.

The self fulfilling prophecy - Once the perpetual lie has been forgotten and neatly tucked away in some inner fold of our psyche, the machine begins a very methodical and extraordinary process of fulfilling "the prophecy." The prophecy is a representation of the original pain. The prophecy is evidence to the machine that indeed that original pain was real and that there is a continuation of this damage and injury to the real self. This, of course, is essential because it continue to justify the machine's existence. It continues to justify our need to have the machine for protection. After all, if we are continually getting "injured" then we must use the continued protection to prevent further disintegration or damage. The machine is incredibly talented and sophisticated in orchestrating events so as to "prove" the fact that the prophecy is real. It might be to prove that all men are no good and capable of abandoning and rejecting you. It may prove that women are indeed castrating and manipulative. It might prove that people can't be trusted and that they will always disappoint you. It will basically prove what your issue is over and over and over and over.

The real self remains hidden – During the course of this gathering of evidence and proving of the prophecy, the real self remains hidden from view in a safe and secure chamber in the vault of privacy deep within the psyche. Of course, it awaits the signals from the machine as to when it is "safe." There are times that the machine allows the real self to come out into the sunlight only to receive a greeting from another's machine in the form of some kind of disappointment, abandonment, rejection, or whatever. Once this is experienced, the real self returns to the protective chamber only to be soothed and nurtured by the machine who lectures it in a way that a parent would tell an adolescent about the "I told you so" argument.

Triggering – Triggering and retriggering strengthen the machine and propagates its' need to survive and cope. Triggering is that process where the machine is activated and has evidence that someone or something in the environment is dangerous, damaging, hurtful, or potentially abusive. When a person is triggered and they believe the lie the machine has told them (the danger is real) and the person allows the machine to cope, then that process strengthens the existence of the machine and the need for further protection.

"Perceived" danger – Perceived danger appears to be authentic. This is validated by the perceived injury and subsequent emotional experience of pain. The real self "believes" the words of the machine that the person or situation is dangerous or harmful. The real self has clearly lost touch with what is genuine danger and what is only perceived danger. In fact, if the machine cannot decide whether something is dangerous or not it takes the conservative approach and treats it as though it is dangerous.

The confrontation – When the real self has been repressed and hidden from view for many, many years and has missed out on the opportunity of intimacy, authentic loving and surrendering, it begins to feel a sense of loss, suffocation and a "slow death." It begins to feel unfulfilled. It lacks motivation, ambition, and creativity. It might be successful because of the efforts of its' machine, but it lacks substance and a connection to what is genuine and rewarding. It is at this point that the real self wants to confront the machine. This is a very difficult and awkward experience because there is a tremendous amount of ambiguity that the real self has in regards to the machine. One might view this as the relationship between parents and an adolescent. The adolescent is beginning to separate and individuate from its' parents and it is indeed grateful to them for all their guidance and protection. However, it wants to be its' own person. In the course of this separation it is sometimes necessary for the adolescent to rebel or assert itself in a rather strong manner in order to break the emotional ties and confines of a doubting mother or father. The separation, if done in a healthy way, is merely a way of letting go and reconnecting in a different way. In other words, the adolescent goes from being a boy to becoming a man. He now has a "friendship" with his father, rather than feeling like he is being infantilized or treated as a child. Parents have a tremendous amount of difficulty letting go because they are fearful that the breaking of the connection might mean a loss forever. So, the more they try to control and stay connected the more some adolescents' rebel. Sometimes it takes a rebellion of anger in order to break loose to become one's own person. In the same sense the real self, when it becomes aware of what has happened to it, wants this type of separation and individualization. Through the Personal Balance ™ Model and Personal Balance™ Therapy, one can be coached through a variety of tools to achieve this separation very successfully. Some patients report that they would like to "kill their machine" or throw it away, or destroy it. This, of course, is not necessary. I am quick to remind patients that they are indeed indebted to their machine for its' tremendous service and faithfulness in providing what the machine has believed to be a form of protection. The machine actually believes its' own lie when it is trying to protect us from what it perceives as to be dangerous. But when the real self risks in an authentic way, it can demonstrate to the machine that what it was believing to be dangerous was, in fact, not dangerous at all. Even though what was outside reminded the machine of the original pain, the real self can now show the machine that there is no danger in the risking and so therefore, there is an opportunity to modify the vigilance and the activation level of the machine.

Continual risking – Through this persistence in risking, the real self educates itself and the machine as to the fact that what the machine was identifying as real danger was, in fact, a lie. It also educates the machine and in a sense can reprogram it. Once this occurs, the real self is empowered and has a sense of freedom that it has never felt before. It now has new energy available to it because it is no longer using a tremendous amount of its' emotional resource to stay hidden. It is letting feelings out rather than using a lot of energy to repress or hold them in. When something occurs in the environment, the real self has a much better perspective and does not take the event personally or believe it to be about them at all. It can show compassion and mercy and undeserved forgiveness to others who are massively triggered or activated.

The internal shift of psychic position where the real self sits in the driver's seat and allows the machine to sit in the passenger's seat is absolutely essential to personal growth and Personal Balance ™. It is also important because the real self becomes empowered to "owning" the machine, rather than the machine owning it. This is

Personal Balance™ in its' truest form. It is the essential balance of the real and protective self. The education and modification of the machine and the reclaiming of the real self to its' rightful place in the psychic structure is the essence of Personal Balance™ and the foundation for achieving enlightenment and a state of grace.

I invite you to begin this road to self discovery and restoration of your inner balance. When you first understand what you have done to yourself and you forgive your machine for doing its' job, then you can reclaim your rightful place inside to really experience the present and begin to live. You can free yourself from the automatic behaviors that have kept you buried deep inside. You can feel the sunlight on your face and the gentle wind in your hair and actually begin to fulfill your destiny. This extraordinary place of Personal Balance™ allows you to create authentic intentions that when watered with faith and guided by the inner cable (God), will answer the question of "why am I here " and "what is life all about."

Your inner balance and alignment, along with your ability to keep your machine from distracting you, will allow the universe to manifest assistance to fulfill your intention.

The creation and fulfillment of an intention makes a contribution to the rest of us and to the planet. Our ultimate Creator is pleased because making authentic intentions crystallize into reality, is the highest compliment we can give God.

Remaining in the state of Personal Balance ™ does take constant work with particular focus on *not* letting the machine wiggle its' way back into power and dominance. There are constant inner comments it will make to try to seduce and distract you and take your focus away. By remaining in faith and belief and keeping connected to the inner cable (God) for direction, you will discover that remaining open and vulnerable is truly a very powerful state. You will discover that your need for the full suit of armor for protection has been reduced to a small pocket knife. You now travel light. . . .light enough to maneuver more efficiently. . . .light enough to fulfill your authentic intentions ….light enough to fulfill your true destiny. . . . see you out there. . . . I'll be the guy flying by on my bike yelling "catch me if you can!"

THE PERSONAL BALANCE™ WORKBOOK

The following workbook is provided to give you a more concrete and structured opportunity to "see" yourself. I have given you a description, using my model, of you and your machine. You now understand that your mind has been lying to you and how this has happened. It's time to forgive your machine and move forward by removing doubt, fear and distraction. This workbook will allow you to start the journey to reclaim yourself and be back in the driver's seat where you belong. Be honest with your answers and try to keep your machine from getting in the way. Take regular time to "water" yourself and welcome any and all feelings that surface. You don't have to understand them or try to analyze them. . . . they just need to be felt. Remember, your authentic is connected to the feelings and as you express the feelings you have more of yourself available. By surrendering to your pain, you re-educate the machine about pain and begin to remove its' fear of it.

What are you afraid of?

I'm afraid of:

_____

_____

_____

_____

_____

I'm afraid that:

_____

_____

_____

_____

_____

Who really and truly knows you?

_____

_____

_____

_____

_____

When was the last time you cried?

_____

_____

_____

_____

_____

Why did you cry?

_____

_____

_____

_____

_____

What emotions are hard for you to feel or express?

_____

_____

_____

_____

_____

Can you tell the difference between when you are being real and when you are being phony?

_____

_____

_____

_____

_____

When two people meet each other for the first time why can't they be real with each other?

_____

_____

_____

_____

_____

What percentage of the time do you believe you are real?

_____

_____

_____

_____

_____

What percentage of the time do you believe you are being the machine or being protected?

_____

_____

_____

_____

_____

What do you resent right now?

_____

_____

_____

_____

_____

What do you do with your anger?

_____

_____

_____

_____

_____

What do you wish for and what do you want?

I wish that:

_____

_____

_____

_____

_____

I want:

_____

_____

_____

_____

_____

Do you believe you treat people the way you secretly would like to be treated?

_____

_____

_____

_____

_____

What in your life are you ashamed of? What do you regret?

_____

_____

_____

_____

_____

What do you like about yourself?

_____

_____

_____

_____

_____

What would you like to improve on?

_____

_____

_____

_____

_____

What is it about intimacy and getting close to someone that frightens you?

_____

_____

_____

_____

_____

When was the last time you did something really special for you? What exactly did you do?

_____

_____

_____

_____

_____

List the excuses you use to **not** exercise.

_____

_____

_____

_____

_____

What are the things that trigger me?

(i.e., people leaving, separations, when people question my feelings, when people make me wrong, insensitivity, unfairness, people not trusting me, people lying to me, people taking me for granted, etc.)

_____

_____

_____

_____

_____

List the ways that I survive

(How the machine protects me – shutting down, withdrawing, going inside myself, being confrontational, using humor, arguing, explaining of justifying myself, etc.)

_____

_____

_____

_____

_____

Original Pain – How I was first injured

SENTENCE COMPLETION

I love it when I

_____

_____

_____

_____

_____

Most men

_____

_____

_____

_____

_____

Most Women

_____

_____

_____

_____

_____

My parents always

_____

_____

_____

_____

_____

I sent

_____

_____

_____

_____

_____

What I am most afraid of is

_____

_____

_____

_____

_____

Most people don't know that I

_____

_____

_____

_____

_____

Children always

_____

_____

_____

_____

_____

No one knows that

_____

_____

_____

_____

_____

I am ashamed of

_____

_____

_____

_____

_____

I know I'm authentic when I

_____

_____

_____

_____

_____

I am sad when

_____

_____

_____

_____

_____

I wish people would

_____
_____
_____
_____
_____

I wish I could

_____
_____
_____
_____
_____

If people knew

_____
_____
_____
_____
_____

They wouldn't like me.

I can remember as far back as

_____
_____
_____
_____
_____

Life is

_____

_____

_____

_____

_____

The last thing I remember the most about being a child is

_____

_____

_____

_____

_____

My dad always

_____

_____

_____

_____

_____

School was

_____

_____

_____

_____

_____

My mom would never

_____

_____

_____

_____

_____

I like the way I

_____

_____

_____

_____

_____

God is

_____

_____

_____

_____

_____

What I really want is

_____

_____

_____

_____

_____

What I like the most about myself is

_____

_____

_____

_____

_____

I wish I could change my

_____

_____

_____

_____

_____

The world needs

_____

_____

_____

_____

_____

If you want the real me to come out you must

_____

_____

_____

_____

_____

The thing that triggers me the most is

_____

_____

_____

_____

_____

The person who really and truly knows me is

_____

_____

_____

_____

_____

MY MACHINE

Blames others

Justifies and explains

Is defensive – lives in "fear"

Always sees the negative – interprets my pain

Always asks "why"

Always want to "know"

Always is analyzing

Has been there since childhood (my twin)

Wants to medicate my pain

Can actually "sound" authentic – a charmer

Likes power and control

Gets angry quickly

Is suspicious

Doesn't trust – feels betrayed

Keeps files of all the people who have hurt me

Is afraid of getting what it wants **and** is afraid of not getting what it wants

Wants to "get"

Other descriptions of my machine:

1. _____

2. _____

3. _____

4. _____

5. _____

6. _____

7. _____

8. _____

9. _____

10. _____

MY AUTHENTIC

Is loving

Is forgiving

Is kind

Is considerate

Is really me. . . who I am

Is creative

Is spontaneous, childlike

Is a free, loving spirit

Trusts

Wants to "give"

Is connected to God

Has wisdom

Doesn't try. . . it just "is"

Lives in faith – doesn't doubt

Wants to serve others

Does things freely – no strings attached

Loves touch

Is nurturing and healing

Feels a connection to nature and all living things

Wants to simplify

Knows the truth

My authentic also:

1. _____

2. _____

3. _____

4. _____

5. _____

6. _____

7. _____

8. _____

9. _____

10. _____

MY GOALS

My intention is:

_____

_____

_____

_____

_____

What I want to accomplish this year:

_____

_____

_____

_____

_____

What I want to accomplish in five years:

_____

_____

_____

_____

_____

AFFIRMATIONS

I will see and feel myself accomplishing my goals.

I have everything I need inside of me to be successful.

I am not afraid of fear. . . . it is my friend.

I already am successful.

I will listen to my feelings every day.

I already am loved.

I have so much of me, I want to give it away to you.

A SIMPLE EXERCISE

Focus your attention, and imagine the smell of fresh cut grass . . . the taste of a lemon. . the sound of seagulls. . .your child's voice. . . bring your attention to your breathing. Stop your machine from thinking about yesterday and today or worrying about tomorrow. . . Just sense the breathing throughout your body. Bring your attention to the present moment. . . . if you feel emotional, welcome the feeling. . . . if you feel sad or hurt, don't let your machine try to analyze why. . . accept it as your friend. . . embrace it. . . become it. . . Rather than think I am in pain, just notice there is pain. . . . notice your breathing now. . . . as your breathing becomes quieter and more regular, you may notice a subtle pause when your inhaling ends before you exhale. . . . this is a moment of stillness.

This is the present . . . . your machine is in neutral . . . . you feel yourself. . . this is the place to plant an authentic intention . . . .one that is out of contribution. . . .see the movie here. . . . practice going here on a regular basis. . . . this is you7r time for you . . . . you can hear and feel God when the machine is not distracted by fear and doubt. . . Tell yourself: I am already loved, I am special and mindful of my gifts. . . . my gifts are to be used for good . . . . no one has power over me. . . I am responsible for my happiness. . . I do not choose to stay in the negativity of my machine . . . my mind works for me. . .I am in charge . . . . I will not give my power away. . . I am not alone . . . the perfect transformation is already taking place. . . . I will not get in my own way. . . . I will witness my dreams. . . . Life is but a dream. . . . .

Stay in faith and allow pain to always be your friend. By feeling pain and being aware that you are just getting reactivated, you can remain more present and authentic. Remember to be willing to go first because it will invite others to come out. By you remaining more authentic, you make it safe for others to join you. The end of this book is the beginning of your journey – see you out there!

In his new book, You Can't Trust Your Own Mind, Dr. David French describes a very useful model of emotional development in response to our experiences. He describes how the mind tries to protect us from as much emotional pain as possible. His description of the minds' complex responses leads to how some of the responses truly cannot be trusted. His personal experiences and patient interviews develop an understanding that can help the reader have insight into his own "triggers" and "responses" to emotional pain. This brings the reader to the awareness of how returning to his own "authentic self" brings the most rewarding life experiences. After attaining an understanding of his model, Dr. French's final chapter provides a "workbook" to "seeing ourselves" and moving closer to our own "authentic selves" where we live the most fulfilled lives.

I believe you will find this book fascinating; it will offer the opportunity for honest introspection and a chance to improve our responses to life's difficult experiences.

— **Michael J. Maguire, D.O., Family Practice Physician**

Through transformational stories and effective teaching metaphors Dr. French has helped us to understand how our inherited "overprotective minds" are keeping us from growing into our "authentic" selves. Unwarranted fear is blocking us from evolving into our fully human, loving potential.

Dr. French has written a book that will make you want to live into the vision of who you want to be and show you, step by step, how to become that person.

An inspiring read!

— **Jim McQuire**

M.A. Counseling Psychology, San Francisco State University

To order more Humanics books
please visit our website at

www.humanicspub.com

ISBN 978-0-89334-855-7

90000

PRINTED IN THE UNITED STATES

CPSIA information can be obtained at www.ICGtesting.com
Printed in the USA
LVOW121659301111

257214LV00009B/27/P